Renate Seebauer
NACHHILFE ENGLISCH 2

D1673309

Renate Seebauer

Nachhilfe Englisch

2

Verlag Leitner · Wien

CIP-Kurztitelaufnahme der Deutschen Bibliothek

Seebauer, Renate:
Nachhilfe Englisch / Renate Seebauer. — Wien:
Leitner
   (Leitners Studienhelfer)

2 (1986).
   ISBN 3-85157-047-2

© by Verlag Leitner 1986
in Herold Druck- und Verlagsgesellschaft m.b.H., Wien
Druck : Herold, Wien 8

ISBN 3-85157-047-2

VORWORT

Die vorliegende Handreichung — unter Berücksichtigung der neuen Lehrpläne für Hauptschulen und allgemeinbildende höhere Schulen erstellt — trägt den internationalen Tendenzen im Fremdsprachunterricht voll Rechnung.

Ausgang jeder der 55 Übungseinheiten ist der aktive Sprachgebrauch: Telefongespräche führen, nach dem Weg fragen, Einkaufsgespräche führen, Zustimmung oder Ablehnung ausdrücken, über Vergangenes berichten, Gründe anführen, . . .

Für den aktiven Gebrauch einer Fremdsprache ist die Beherrschung grundlegender grammatikalischer Strukturen Voraussetzung: Did you . . . ? When did he . . . ? . . . bigger than . . . as beautiful as . . . Why . . . ? . . . because . . . If I were . . . , . . .

Diese Verquickung „aktiver Sprachgebrauch" — „grundlegende grammatikalische Strukturen" ist das Grundkonzept von NACHHILFE ENGLISCH 2.

Der Einstieg in die Übungseinheit erfolgt fast ausschließlich über einen Dialog (Gespräch im Kästchen), der kommunikativ relevant ist und vom Schüler sofort in seinen aktiven Sprachgebrauch integriert werden kann.

Im Anschluß daran findet sich eine Vielzahl von Übungen, in welchen die im Dialog vorhandenen grammatikalischen Strukturen schrittweise aufgearbeitet und anhand zahlreicher Beispiele eingeübt werden.

Die Übungseinheiten 1 - 8 dienen der Wiederholung und Festigung des Lehrstoffes der 5. Schulstufe.

Die Übungseinheiten 9 - 55 beziehen sich auf den Lehrstoff der 6. Schulstufe.

Für jeweils acht bis zwölf Übungseinheiten wurden Kontrolltests (TRY THIS TEST) mit leistungsdifferenzierter Auswertung erstellt — eine Rückmeldung für den unmittelbaren Lernerfolg des Schülers.

Alle Übungen sind so angelegt, daß sie sowohl mündlich als auch schriftlich in Einzel-, Partner- oder Gruppenarbeit durchgeführt werden können.

Der vorliegende Band NACHHILFE ENGLISCH 2 gestattet vielfältige Einsatzmöglichkeiten:

— Das häusliche Wiederholen und Üben wird sinnvoll unterstützt.

— Der schulische Förderunterricht wird um eine Vielzahl von Übungsmöglichkeiten bereichert.

— Durch die ausgeführten Lösungen erhält der Schüler Rückmeldung über seinen Leistungsstand.

Somit stellt NACHHILFE ENGLISCH 2 ein besonderes Übungsangebot dar.

Wien, im Jänner 1986   Renate Seebauer

ACTIVITY
IS THE ONLY ROAD
TO KNOWLEDGE
(G. B. Shaw)

INHALTSVERZEICHNIS

Übungs-einheit	Arbeitstitel	Übungsschwerpunkt (Grammatik)
13	TITTLE-TATTLE	„Nicht wahr?" (mit Haupt zeitwort)
14	WHY NOT? . . . BECAUSE . . .	Satzverbindung mit „weil"
15	DON'T BE SO NOSY!	Fragebildung „Warum?" Satzverbindung mit „weil"
16	AT THE TRAVEL AGENCY	Satzverbindung „so / aus diesem Grund" (that's why)
17	WHAT CAN WE PLAY THIS AFTERNOON?	Englisches Alphabet / Buchstabieren
18	AN INTERVIEW AT THE AIRPORT	Fragebildung (Mitvergangenheit)
19	CAN YOU TELL ME THE WAY TO . . . PLEASE?	Wortschatz / Strukturen „nach dem Weg fragen"
20	HOW DO YOU GET TO SCHOOL?	Umstandswörter: oft, nie, gewöhnlich, manch-mal . . . / **by** bus, **by** car, . . .
21	HOW LONG DOES IT TAKE YOU . . .?	Zeitangaben (an hour, half an hour, . . .) Brauchen: need, it takes me
	TRY THIS TEST	(Kontrolltest über die Übungseinheiten 9–21)
22	AS COLD AS . . . AS HOT AS . . . AS WARM AS . . .	Vergleiche: so–wie (as–as)

Übungs-einheit	Arbeitstitel	Übungsschwerpunkt (Grammatik)
23	WINDOW-SHOPPING	Steigerung des Eigenschaf[t]worts (-er, -est / more, mos[t])
24	TALKING ABOUT THE WEATHER	Unregelmäßige Steigerunge[n]
25	I AM STRONGER THAN YOU	Vergleiche: -er than
26	WHAT DO THE WEATHERMEN SAY?	Dem Wetterbericht einer Tageszeitung Sinn entnehm[en]
27	THE FORTUNE-TELLER WILL TELL YOU THE FUTURE	Zukunft (will-future)
28	IN A DEPARTMENT STORE 1	Zukunft (will) ≠ want
29	CLEARANCE SALES! EVERYTHING'S REDUCED!	Zukunft (Signalwörter: next, tomorrow,...)
30	SHOPPING IN THE BURLINGTON ARCADES	Stützwort: one – ones
31	LET'S DO THE SHOPPING	Mengenangaben: a box **of**, a bottle **of**,... some – any
32	WHO OR WHICH?	bezügliche Fürwörter: who – which
33	IN A DEPARTMENT STORE 2	„passen": fit, suit, go with
34	WHAT WAS GOING ON WHEN...?	Dauerform der Mitverga-genheit (was / were playing) Satzverbindungen: while / when

13

Übungs-einheit	Arbeitstitel	Übungsschwerpunkt (Grammatik)
	TRY THIS TEST	(Kontrolltest über die Übungseinheiten 22–34)
35	A MESS IN THE CLASSROOM	„Saxon Genitive" / „Possessive Case": mine, yours…
36	DIFFERENT SCHOOLS – THE SAME LESSONS	Unterrichtsgegenstände / once, twice, three times…
37	A LETTER FROM ENGLAND	Englisches Schulwesen / gern – lieber – am liebsten
38	HAVE YOU DONE YOUR EXERCISES YET?	Vergangenheit (Present Perfect Tense)
39	SIGHTSEEING IN LONDON	Vergangenheit / Signal-wörter: ever, never, just, already
40	EVERYTHING HERE'S SECOND-HAND!	Vergangenheit
41	SKIING IN SPRING	Umstandswort (Adverb)
42	A COMPETITION	Steigerung des Umstandswortes
43	A NEW PUPIL	Vergangenheit – Mitver-gangenheit (Signalwörter: ever, never, ago, last)
44	HOW TO MAKE A CAKE	Backrezept verstehen / Vergangenheit
45	IT'S THE BEST FILM THAT I'VE EVER SEEN	Bezügliches Fürwort THAT
	TRY THIS TEST	(Kontrolltest über die Übungseinheiten 35–45)

PEN FRIENDS ALL OVER THE WORLD

Betty: Look! I've got a lot of names and addresses of pen friends in Europe, America and Australia!

Mary White, 12
Hobbies: languages, stamps
63, Steelcase Road West,
Markham, Ontario
CANADA

James Greene, 13
Hobbies: reading books,
writing letters
46, Park Street,
Ringwood, Victoria
AUSTRALIA

Anna and Maria Ferrari, 13
Hobbies: taking photos,
swimming
Via Obizzi 69
Roma
ITALY

Sue Hawthorne, 13
Hobbies: singing, travelling
44, Glenageary Rd.
Dublin
IRELAND

Hans Meier, 12
Hobbies: music, animals
Schloßgasse 45
A-3580 Horn
AUSTRIA

Jane: Let me see!
Oh, I'd like
an Austrian pen friend!
Betty: And I'd like an
Australian pen friend.
Jane: Be careful!
Don't mix up Austria
and Australia!

If you wish to have pen friends
all over the world, write to . . .

1. Lies das Gespräch im Kästchen gut durch; dann beantworte folgende Fragen!

a) Who wants an Austrian pen friend?
b) Who wants an Australian pen friend?
c) Where does Mary White live?

d) How old is Hans Meier?
e) Do Anna and Maria live in Austria?
f) What do you know about Sue's hobbies?

2. *Bilde anhand der Anzeigen Sätze nach folgendem Muster!*
   Beachte die Fürwörter!

Mary is twelve years old.
She lives in Canada.
Her hobbies are languages and collecting stamps.

---

a) James . . .   c) Sue . . .
b) Hans . . .   d) Anna and Maria . . .

3. *Ergänze die fehlenden Fürwörter!*

a) **Tom** wants to write a letter. . . . writes a
   letter to Mary. Mary is . . . pen friend.
b) **Jim and I** want to have pen friends in Italy,
   so . . . write to Anna and Maria. Anna
   and Maria are . . . pen friends.
c) **Ann and Joe** are going to write a card to
   James. So . . . are going to write to
   Australia.
d) **Nelly** wants an Irish pen friend. . . . is
   going to write to Sue.
e) **Nelly's** pen friend is Sue. . . . pen friend
   lives in Ireland.
f) **Peter's** pen friend is 13 years old. . . . pen
   friend lives in England.
g) **Susan's** pen friend is 12 years old. . . . pen
   friend lives in Austria.

Beachte!

I   - my
you`- your
he   - his
she   - her
we   - our
you - your
they - their

4. *Versuche selbst eine Anzeige!*

_____ , _____

Hobbies: _____
_____

---

a) What's your name?   c) What are your hobbies?
b) How old are you?   d) Where do you live?

2 A GUESSING GAME

Peter:	I'm thinking of something. What is it?		
Tom: Peter:	No, it	Is isn't	it a person? .
Tom: Peter:	Yes, it	Is is	it a thing? .
Tom: Peter:	No, you	Can can't	I see it in the classroom? .
Tom: Peter:	Yes, you	Can can	I play with it? .
Tom: Peter:	Yes, I	Have have	you got such a thing? .
Tom: Peter:	Yes, I	Do do	you like to play with it? .
Tom: Peter:	Yes, it	Is is	it a toy train? .

1. *Lies das Ratespiel im Kästchen gut durch!*
Beachte jeweils das **Zeitwort** *in der* **Frage** *und in der* **Kurzantwort!**

2. *Ergänze die Kurzantwort! Beachte "have", "has"!*

a) Have you got a lot of work to do? Yes, ...
b) Has Tom got new shoes? No, ...
c) Have Joe and Mary got new satchels? Yes, ...
d) Have you got many books? No, ...
e) Has Nelly got a nice room? Yes, ...
f) Have the children got many toys? Yes, ...

3. Ergänze die Kurzantwort! Beachte "am, is, are"!

a) Are the children singing songs? Yes, . . .
b) Is Peter doing his homework? No, . . .
c) Are you playing football? Yes, . . .
d) Are the children writing their exercises? Yes, . . .
e) Is Mary reading a book? No, . . .
f) Are you learning English? Yes, . . .

4. Ergänze die Kurzantwort! Beachte "do, does, did"!

a) Do you like porridge? Yes, . . .
b) Does Jim play the guitar? No, . . .
c) Did Ann learn French? No, . . .
d) Do Tom and Ann sing English songs? Yes, . . .
e) Did Jack go by bus? No, . . .
f) Does Mary eat biscuits? Yes, . . .

5. Ergänze jeweils die Kurzantwort!

a) Are you a pupil?
b) Do you go to school in Vienna?
c) Can you play tennis?
d) Does your friend like to read books?
e) Have you got a lot of toys?
f) Do you like to go to school?
g) Is your friend a good pupil?
h) Has your friend got new school things?
i) Did you spend your holidays in England?
j) Did you ask your teacher yesterday?
k) Can your friend play football?
l) Are you a boy?

6. Versuche mit deinem Partner ein ähnliches Ratespiel wie zu Beginn des Kapitels!
Sieger ist, wer die wenigsten Fragen stellen muß.

Beginne: I'm thinking of something.
What is it?

Sue: I've got to put [these] pencils into my pencil-case.

Jack: And what about [those] pens over there?

Sue: I think they belong to you.
[These] here are my pens, [those] over there are your pens.

Jack: And what about [that] book on the shelf over there?

Sue: [This] here is my book, [that] book over there belongs to you.

Sue and Jack: And what about y o u r school things?

Beachte!
Hinweisende Fürwörter!

(Einzahl) THIS   (Einzahl) THAT
(Mehrzahl) THESE   (Mehrzahl) THOSE
↓   ↓
. . . **nahe**   . . . **entfernt**
dem Sprecher   vom Sprecher

1. Bilde Sätze nach folgendem Muster!

This book here belongs to me,
that book over there belongs to you.

Verwende: fountain-pen, ruler, satchel, pencil-case, copy-book, . . .

2. Bilde Sätze nach folgendem Muster!

These books here belong to me,
those books over there belong to you.

Verwende: fountain-pens, rulers, satchels, pencil-cases, copy-books, . . .

3. *Bilde Minidialoge nach folgendem Muster!*

> Mum: What about these pencils here?
> Sue: I think these pencils belong to Jack, those pencils over there belong to me.

Verwende: ball-pens, books, rubbers, pencil-sharpeners, triangles, . . .

4. *Bilde möglichst viele Dialoge!*

A:	This These	books pencils ruler copy-books pencil-sharpener	belongs belong	to me.

B:	That Those	over there	is are	your	books. pencils. ruler. copy-books. pencil-sharpener.

5. *Ergänze die Lücken!*

a) . . . satchel here belongs to me.
b) . . . books over there are Tom's.
c) . . . pencils here are Betty's.
d) What about . . . exercise-book here?
e) I think . . . rulers here are Jim's.
f) And what about . . . rulers over there?

Ann: This is Ann speaking.

Betty: Hello, Ann! What are you doing?

Ann: I'm ⬚just⬚ doing my English exercises.

      I ⬚always⬚ do my English exercises in the afternoon.

Betty: I'm ⬚just⬚ writing a letter to Austria.

      I ⬚always⬚ write a letter to Austria on Wednesday afternoon.
      And what is your brother John doing?

Ann: He is playing on the piano ⬚at the moment⬚ .

      He ⬚often⬚ plays on the piano in the afternoon.

Betty: It's a pity that everyone is busy. I'm afraid we can't go out this afternoon! Bye, bye!

Ann: Good-bye, Betty!

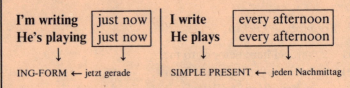

Beachte!

| **I'm writing** | just now | **I write** | every afternoon |
| **He's playing** | just now | **He plays** | every afternoon |

ING-FORM ← jetzt gerade   SIMPLE PRESENT ← jeden Nachmittag

Die Handlung (Tätigkeit)

geht **im Augenblick des Sprechens** vor sich. | bezeichnet einen **wiederholten** (immer wiederkehrenden) **Vorgang.**

1. *Bilde Sätze nach folgendem Muster!*

> **I'm singing** a song **just now.**
> **I always sing** a song in the morning.

a) write a letter . . . / . . . in the evening
b) play football . . . / . . . in the afternoon
c) drink tea . . . / . . . in the morning
d) eat a piece of cake . . . / . . . in the afternoon

2. *Bilde Sätze nach folgendem Muster!*

> **Tom is singing** a song **just now.**
> **He always sings** a song in the morning.

Verwende die Angaben von Aufgabe 1!

3. *Lies das Telefongespräch im Kästchen gut durch!*
   Versuche ähnliche Gespräche!

a) Sue: . . . learn French
   Joe: . . . study mathematics . . . / sister Betty
   Sue: . . . go for a walk

b) Jack: . . . read a book
   John: . . . make my bed . . . / brother Pat
   Jack: . . . do his homework

4. *Ergänze jeweils die richtige Form des Zeitworts!*

a) run: Look! The boys . . .
          They . . . to school every morning.

b) sing: Listen! Betty . . . an American song.
          She often . . . American songs.

c) dance: Ann and Pat always . . . in the evening.
          Look! They . . . just now.

d) eat: Peter often . . . an apple.
          Yes, he . . . an apple again.

5 | TEA-TIME

Mrs Brown: Would you like a cup of tea, Mrs White?

Mrs White: Oh yes, please! I like tea but I don't like coffee.

Mrs Brown: And what about some cake?

Mrs White: Oh yes, I like a piece of cake but I don't like biscuits.

Mrs Brown: And your little daughter? Does she drink tea and does she eat a piece of cake?

Mrs White: Yes, of course!
She drinks tea but she doesn't drink milk!
She doesn't eat cakes and she doesn't eat biscuits! Naughty Lucy!

Beachte die Verneinung (Hauptzeitwort im Satz)!

Nach dem Satzgegenstand wird DO NOT (= DON'T) / DOES NOT (= DOESN'T) eingeschoben, gefolgt vom Hauptzeitwort in der Nennform.

I / you we / you / they	DO NOT (= DON'T)	+ Infinitive (Nennform)
He / she / it	DOES NOT (= DOESN'T)	

1. *Bilde Sätze nach folgendem Muster!*

I like ham but **I don't like** bacon.

a) bread / cakes   d) juice / beer
b) jelly / porridge   e) milk / wine
c) cornflakes / biscuits f) cocoa / whisky

2. Bilde möglichst viele Sätze!

I			go to school.
Peter	don't		help in the kitchen.
Sue and Ellen	doesn't	want to	eat ice-cream.
Mary			go to the cinema.

3. Bilde Minidialoge nach folgendem Muster!

A: Does your <u>brother</u> (1) <u>drink</u> (2) <u>tonic water</u>? (3)
B: Of course, he does! (4)
   But he doesn't drink <u>wine</u>.

(1)	(2)	(3)	(4)
a) sister	eat	rolls	bread
b) girl friend	drink	coffee	cocoa
c) father	like	beer	wine
d) mother	eat	cakes	biscuits

4. Ergänze jeweils die Kurzantwort!

a) Do you like gin? No, . . .
b) Does your girl friend like biscuits? Yes, . . .
c) Do you drink wine? No, . . .
d) Do Jack and Joe eat cornflakes? No, . . .
e) Do all the children drink beer? No, . . .
f) Does your brother like whisky? No, . . .
g) Does Mr Miller drink wine? Yes, . . .
h) Do all the girls like sweets? No, . . .

5. Lies den Dialog im Kästchen nochmals gut durch!
   Versuche ähnliche Gespräche!

6 LITTLE SUSY ALWAYS ASKS QUESTIONS

Susy:	Where ☐are☐ you, Mum?
Mum:	Here I am, Susy!
Susy:	What ☐are☐ you doing, Mum?
Mum:	I'm preparing lunch.
Susy:	Mum, ☐can☐ you play with me?
Mum:	Sorry, dear, I can't play with you now!
Susy:	When ☐do☐ you go shopping?
Mum:	I always go shopping in the afternoon - don't you know?
Susy:	Where ☐are☐ you going to, Mum? Who ☐is☐ that man in our garden? What . . ., where . . . , when . . . ?
Mum:	Oh Susy! I can't answer all your questions!

Where? Wo?

What? Was?

When? Wann?

Where . . . to? Wohin?

Who? Wer?

Beachte bei der Fragebildung das ☐Hilfszeitwort☐ :
IS, ARE, CAN, . . . bzw. DO / DOES, wenn noch ein **Hauptzeitwort** folgt!

1. *Bilde WHO-Fragen nach folgendem Muster!*

Tom ☐is☐ at home.	Who ☐is☐ at home?
Tom ☐writes☐ a letter.	Who ☐writes☐ a letter?

a) Peter is in the garden.
b) Ann can sing English songs.
c) Sue reads German books.
d) Pat plays in the garden.

e) Sandy asks the teacher.
f) Jane learns English.
g) Mary is at school.
h) Joe can swim.

2. *Bilde WHERE-Fragen nach folgendem Muster!*

Tom ⬚is⬚ at home.	Where ⬚is⬚ Tom?
Tom ⬚plays⬚ in the garden.	Where ⬚does⬚ Tom play?

a) Peter is <u>in the garden.</u>
b) Jane plays <u>in the park.</u>
c) Pat runs <u>to the cinema.</u> Where . . . to?
d) Sandy can go <u>to her friend.</u>
e) Joe is <u>at the cinema.</u>
f) Sue goes <u>to school.</u>
g) Mary helps <u>in the house.</u>
h) Ann writes her exercises <u>at school.</u>

3. *Bilde WHEN-Fragen nach folgendem Muster!*

Tom ⬚can⬚ come at 4.	When ⬚can⬚ Tom come?
Tom ⬚comes⬚ at 4.	When ⬚does⬚ Tom come?

a) Peter can go <u>at 2.</u>
b) Jane goes to school <u>at 8.</u>
c) Pat comes home <u>at 3.</u>
d) Sandy does her exercises <u>at 6.</u>
e) Joe is at home <u>between 2 and 4.</u>
f) Sue may leave <u>at 7.</u>
g) Mary reads her books in <u>the evening.</u>
h) Ann works <u>in the afternoon.</u>

4. *Welche Fragen hat "Little Susy" gestellt?*

Susy asks Mum where Dad is.
Susy: Where is Dad, Mum?

a) Susy asks Mum when Dad can come.
b) Susy asks Mum what Dad is writing.
c) She asks Mum where her ball is.
d) She asks Mum where she can play.
e) She asks Mum when she can play in the garden.
f) She asks Mum where she is working.

29

Joe: Hello, Fred! Where did you spend your summer holidays?	to spend - [spent]
	to stay - stay<u>ed</u>
Fred: I <u>spent</u> my holidays in Austria. I <u>stayed</u> in Salzburg. When the weather <u>was</u> fine I <u>went</u> sailing. When the weather <u>was</u> bad I <u>went</u> sightseeing. I <u>liked</u> climbing best. We <u>returned</u> home in August.	to go - [went]
	to be - [was / were]
	to like - like<u>d</u>
Joe: I think you <u>had</u> a good time! I <u>spent</u> my holidays with the scouts in Scotland. There <u>were</u> 28 boys in our camp, so we <u>had</u> a lot of fun. I <u>arrived</u> a week ago. But now I must hurry. Bye, bye, Fred!	to return - return<u>ed</u>
	to have - [had]
	to arrive - arriv<u>ed</u>
Fred: So long — see you tomorrow!	

Beachte die Bildung der **Mitvergangenheit**!

Regelmäßige Zeitwörter:
  to like → liked ⎫
  to look → looked ⎭ . . .Nennform + **ed**

Unregelmäßige Zeitwörter:
  to go → [went] ⟍ . . . selbständige
  to have → [had] ⟋ "Past Tense-Form"

1. Bilde möglichst viele sinnvolle Sätze!

When the weather was	fine bad	I Tom Sue	went swimming. watched TV. wrote postcards. played outdoor games.

2. Bilde Sätze nach folgendem Muster!

> I **liked** playing football best,
> so I often **played** football.

a) Ann / playing tennis
b) Tom / climbing mountains
c) Sue / picking mushrooms
d) Joe and Jack / riding on horseback
e) Nelly and Fred / drinking Coke
f) Sandy / going to the country

3. Bilde Minidialoge nach folgendem Muster!

> Tom: Let's **play** football!
> Pat: Oh no, we **played** football yesterday!

a) climb mountains
b) play tennis
c) pick mushrooms
d) drink Coke
e) ride on horseback
f) go to the country

4. Beantworte folgende Fragen in der Mitvergangenheit!

a) Where did you spend your summer holidays?
b) With whom did you stay?
c) How long did you stay?
d) What did you do when the weather was bad?
e) What did you do when the weather was fine?
f) What did you like best?
g) What did you see in the country (in town, at the seaside)?
h) When did you return home?

5. Berichte über deine Ferien und achte auf die Mitvergangenheit!

Verwende: spend, stay, go, see, like, have, play, return ...

8 LAST SUMMER — EVERY SUMMER

Joe: Hello, Fred! When did you come back from your summer holidays?

Fred: I came back on the fifteenth of August.
I always **come** back in August.
Where did you spend your holidays?

Joe: I spent my holidays in Italy.
We usually **spend** our summer holidays in Italy.
We went swimming and boating.

Fred: Oh, I know! You often **go** swimming when the weather is fine. Last summer I wrote many picture postcards to my friends in England.

Joe: You usually **write** a picture postcard to me in summer. What about last summer? Did you forget to write to me?

Beachte!

Gegenwart (Present Tense): bezeichnet einen **wiederholten Vorgang** (always, usually, every day, every summer, . . .)

Mitvergangenheit (Past Tense) : bezeichnet eine **abgeschlossene Handlung** (last summer, last week, two years ago, . . . yesterday, . . .)

1. *Lies den Dialog im Kästchen gut durch!*
   Beachte jeweils "Present Tense" – "Past Tense"!

2. *Bilde Minidialoge nach folgendem Muster!*

A: Did you play outdoor games last summer?
B: Yes, I **played** outdoor games. I usually **play** outdoor games in summer.

a) Did you go sightseeing last summer?
b) Did you read books last summer?
c) Did you eat ice-cream last summer?
d) Did you travel to Austria last summer?
e) Did you pick flowers last summer?

3. "Present Tense" oder "Past Tense"? Ergänze das Zeitwort!

to play: Last summer Tom . . . tennis.
He often . . . tennis when the weather is fine.

to write: Jim . . . his exercises in the afternoon.
Yesterday he . . . his exercises in the evening.

to go: Every Tuesday Peter . . . swimming.
Yesterday was Tuesday: he . . . swimming.

to come: On Monday Ann . . . home at 4.
Yesterday was Monday, so she . . . home at 4.

to read: Last month Tom . . . three books.
He often . . . books in the evening.

to eat: Yesterday I . . . five apples.
In summer I . . . many apples.

4. Freds Urlaubskarte an Joe:

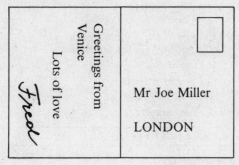

a) What's wrong with Fred's picture postcard?

b) Why did Joe not get this card?

c) Did y o u write all your picture postcards correctly?

TRY THIS TEST

UNIT 1-8

A. *Streiche den Buchstaben v o r dem Wort durch, das in die Lücke paßt!*

> Last winter Joe . . . skiing.
> a) go   b) goes   c) to go   d̸) went

1. Every summer the children . . . to Italy.
   a) travels   b) travelled   c) travel   d) is travelling

2. On Monday Peter often . . . swimming.
   a) goes   b) went   c) go   d) doesn't go

3. Look! Tom . . . his exercises.
   a) are doing   b) does   c) am doing   d) is doing

4. Last summer Joe . . . in London.
   a) was   b) weren't   c) were   d) is

5. Yesterday Pat . . . two letters to Austria.
   a) writes   b) write   c) doesn't write   d) wrote

6. Last winter the children . . . in Austria.
   a) wasn't   b) was   c) are   d) were

7. Listen! The children . . . an English song.
   a) sing   b) sings   c) is singing   d) are singing

8. Every morning Tom . . . to school.
   a) run   b) runs   c) are running   d) is running

9. Tom and Ann . . . in the garden now.
   a) is playing   b) play   c) are playing   d) plays

10. During his last summer holidays Joe . . . four letters.
    a) wrote   b) writes   c) write   d) is writing

11. Peter . . . his last holidays in Italy.
    a) spends   b) spent   c) spend   d) is spending

12. Where are the children? They . . . in the garden now.
    a) playing   b) is playing   c) are playing   d) played

points: ⎕12

B. *Ergänze jeweils die Kurzantwort!*

> Is Peter playing in the park? Yes, *he is* .

1. Can you play football? Yes, . . .
2. Are your friends at school now? No, . . .
3. Are you a good pupil? Yes, . . .
4. Do you get up at 7? Yes, . . .
5. Does your girl friend speak English? Yes, . . .
6. Have you got new school things? Yes, . . .
7. Has Jim got a new pen? No, . . .
8. Did Tom spend his holidays in England? Yes, . . .

points: ⎕8

C.   Ergänze das Fragefürwort!

> Tom was in England. *Who* was in England?

1. Peter spent his holidays **in England.** . . . did he spend his holidays?
2. Jane studied **English.** . . . did she study?
3. Joe comes home **at 4.** . . . does he come home?
4. **Ann** wrote 6 letters. . . . wrote six letters?
5. **The children** were at home. . . . was at home?
6. Mary gets up **at 6.** . . . does she get up?   points: ☐6☐

D.   Kreuze die richtige Form der Verneinung an!

	don't	doesn't
Jane . . . learn English.	☐	☒
1. Peter . . . speak French.	☐	☐
2. Tom and Ann . . . like porridge.	☐	☐
3. The children . . . play in the park.	☐	☐
4. I . . . learn English on Sunday.	☐	☐
5. We . . . like to write letters.	☐	☐
6. Jane . . . sing English songs.	☐	☐

points: ☐6☐

E.   Setze die fehlenden Fürwörter ein!

> Peter can't find *his* shoes. Where are *they*?

1. Ann can't find . . . book. Where is . . . ?
2. The children aren't doing . . . exercises. . . . are in the park.
3. Joe doesn't wash . . . face. . . . is a naughty boy.
4. Where are . . ., Nelly? Here . . . am, Mum!
5. Where are my pencils? I can't find . . . — . . . are in your satchel.

points: ☐10☐

A. - E.: ☐42☐

	very good	more revision needed
AHS, LG1	38 points and more	not even 32 points
LG 2	34 points and more	not even 28 points
LG 3	30 points and more	not even 24 points

9 | HOLIDAY WEATHER

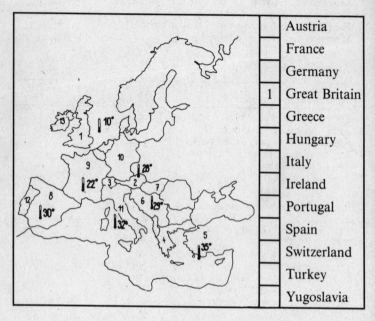

	Austria
	France
	Germany
1	Great Britain
	Greece
	Hungary
	Italy
	Ireland
	Portugal
	Spain
	Switzerland
	Turkey
	Yugoslavia

1. *Ordne die Zahlen auf der Landkarte den Ländernamen zu!*

   Sprich dazu: Number 1 is Great Britain . . .

2. *Bilde Minidialoge nach folgendem Muster!*

Teacher: Where did you spend your holidays, Jack?

Jack: I spent my holidays in Spain.
            It **was** sunny and very nice.
            The temperatures **were** about 30° C.

---

a) Joe: in France / cloudy / quite nice
b) Nelly: in Austria / sunny / very warm
c) Peter: in Italy / sunny / hot
d) Riza: in Turkey / sunny / very hot
e) Anica: in Yugoslavia / cloudy / quite warm

3. *Welche Hauptstadt gehört zu welchem Land? Ordne die richtige Zahl zu!*

1	Austria		Paris	7	Italy		Ankara
2	France		London	8	Ireland		Dublin
3	Germany		Athens	9	Portugal		Berne
4	Greece		Budapest	10	Spain		Rome
5	Hungary		Vienna	11	Switzerland		Madrid
6	Great Britain		Bonn	12	Turkey		Belgrad
				13	Yugoslavia		Lisbon

4. *Bilde Sätze nach folgendem Muster!*

Vienna is the capital of Austria.

Verwende die Angaben von Nr. 3!

5. *Bilde Dialoge nach folgendem Muster!*

Pat: I **was** in Spain.
Joe: And did you see Madrid?
Pat: Yes, we **were** in Madrid, too.

a) Sue: France   d) Riza: Turkey
b) Nelly: Austria   e) Anica: Yugoslavia
c) Peter: Italy   f) Jane: Great Britain

6. *Bilde anhand der Zeitungsmeldung Dialoge nach folgendem Muster!*

A: What **was** the weather like in Athens on the fifteenth of September?
B: It **was** sunny. The temperatures **were** about 28° C.

Athens .... 28° s	Madrid .... 25° s	s = sunny
Budapest ..... 15° c	Paris ...... 18° c	c = cloudy
Dublin .... 12° r	Rome ..... 26° s	r = rainy
London ...... 11° r	Vienna .... 21° s	

10 | JUMBLED SENTENCES

1. Ann <u>spent</u> her holidays at the seaside in Greece.	
2. At the beginning of September her holidays <u>were</u> over and Ann <u>travelled</u> back to London.	
3. Athens <u>was</u> very interesting.	
4. She <u>arrived</u> in London on the third of September.	
5. Once she <u>went</u> to Athens and <u>saw</u> the Acropolis.	
6. The weather <u>was</u> fine all the time, so she <u>went</u> swimming every day.	

Beachte!

Wird über Vergangenes berichtet, das bereits abgeschlossen ist, muß die **Past Tense (Mitvergangenheit)** verwendet werden.

1. Bringe die Sätze der Feriengeschichte in die richtige Reihenfolge!

2. Trage die "Past Tense-Formen" dieser Geschichte und die dazugehörigen Nennformen in diese Tabelle ein!

Past Tense	Infinitive	Past Tense	Infinitive
spent	to spend		

3. *Als die Ansichtskarte aus Griechenland in London ankam, waren manche Wörter nicht mehr lesbar. Trotzdem kannst du den Inhalt der Karte verstehen!*

Dear Susan,
 	
Greetings from . . . !
The . . . is fine, so
I can . . . . . . Yesterday I
. . . . . . Athens to
. . . the Acropolis. Athens
is very . . .
Give my love to . . . . . .
 	
      Yours,
         Ann
	☐.
	
	Miss Susan Miller
	49, Park Lane
	LONDON
	Great Britain

4. *Was hättest du von deinem Urlaubsort geschrieben?*

   Verwende: weather (fine / bad)
                 swimming, play tennis, go sightseeing,
                 interesting, . . .

5. *Übernimm bei folgendem Telefongespräch die Rolle von Ann!*

Betty: Hello, Ann! This is Betty speaking!
Ann: . . .

Betty: Where did you spend your holidays?
Ann: . . .

Betty: Did you see the Acropolis in Athens?
Ann: . . .

Betty: What about the weather?
Ann: . . .

Betty: When did you come back to London?
Ann: . . .

Betty: I'd like to invite you to tea for tomorrow. I hope you
        can come.
Ann: . . . nice of you, thank you!

Ann: Hello, Susan! Did you go swimming or sight-seeing during your holidays?

Susan: I didn't go swimming. I went sightseeing. I didn't stay at the seaside. I stayed in town. And what about you, Ann?

Ann: I played tennis, but I didn't play baseball. I stayed in the country, I didn't stay in town.

Susan: I'd like to know what all the other children did and didn't do during the holidays!

Ann: Let's ask them!

Beachte die **Verneinung in der Mitvergangenheit!**
Nach dem **Satzgegenstand** wird DID NOT (= DIDN'T) eingeschoben, gefolgt vom **Hauptzeitwort in der Nennform.**

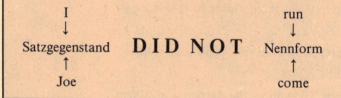

1. *Lies den Dialog im Kästchen gut durch und beachte die Verneinung!*

2. *Bilde Minidialoge nach folgendem Muster!*

A: Did you play tennis or football?
B: I didn't play tennis, I played football.

a) Did you go sightseeing or swimming?
b) Did you play baseball or table-tennis?
c) Did you travel to Italy or to Greece?
d) Did you go by plane or by car?
e) Did you visit Rome or Florence?
f) Did you arrive at Stansted or at Heathrow?

3. *Bilde Sätze nach folgendem Muster!*

> The children **didn't sing** songs during the holidays.

Verwende: learn English, write exercises, play on the piano, help Mum, clean their rooms, work in the garden

4. *Bilde Sätze nach folgendem Muster!*

> Tom **saw** St. Paul's Cathedral.
> Little Joe **didn't see** St. Paul's Cathedral.

a) Tom went to Regent's Park.
b) Tom crossed Oxford Street.
c) He bought fine things.
d) He saw Tower Bridge.
e) He took a photo of the Houses of Parliament.
f) He heard Big Ben.

5. *Ergänze jeweils die "Past Tense" und die "verneinte Past Tense"!*

to go: He . . . to London but he . . . to Oxford.
to write: He . . . letters but he . . . postcards.
to read: We . . . books but we . . . the newspaper.
to sing: She . . . English songs but she . . . Austrian songs.
to take: She . . . her umbrella but she . . . her raincoat.

YOU CAN COME, CAN'T YOU?

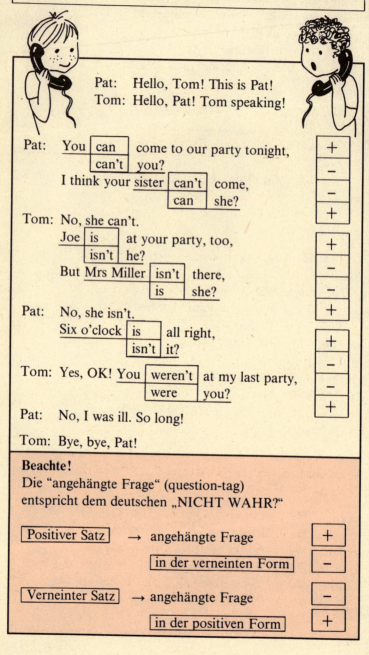

Pat: Hello, Tom! This is Pat!

Tom: Hello, Pat! Tom speaking!

Pat: You | can / can't | come to our party tonight, you? `+` `−`

I think your sister | can't / can | come, she? `−` `+`

Tom: No, she can't.

Joe | is / isn't | at your party, too, he? `+` `−`

But Mrs Miller | isn't / is | there, she? `−` `+`

Pat: No, she isn't.

Six o'clock | is / isn't | all right, it? `+` `−`

Tom: Yes, OK! You | weren't / were | at my last party, you? `−` `+`

Pat: No, I was ill. So long!

Tom: Bye, bye, Pat!

Beachte!

Die "angehängte Frage" (question-tag)
entspricht dem deutschen „NICHT WAHR?"

| Positiver Satz | → angehängte Frage | `+` |

| | in der verneinten Form | `−` |

| Verneinter Satz | → angehängte Frage | `−` |

| | in der positiven Form | `+` |

1. Ergänze jeweils „Nicht wahr?"!

a) Peter **is** a good boy, . . . ?
b) Joe **wasn't** at your party, . . . ?
c) Betty **can** read English books, . . . ?
d) Ann **can't** write, . . . ?
e) The children **were** at school, . . . ?
f) Tom and Sue **weren't** at home, . . . ?
g) The children **are** in the garden, . . . ?
h) You **aren't** lazy, . . . ?
i) Jane **hasn't** got a new pullover, . . .?
j) You **have** got a lot of work to do, . . .?

2. Bilde Dialoge!

A:

This is	my	books,	isn't it?
These are	your	pen,	aren't they?
		pullover,	
		shoes,	

B:

| Yes, | it is. |
| | they are. |

3. Die Engländer sprechen gerne über das Wetter!

	First man:	Second man:
	It's very warm today, isn't it?	Yes, it is.
a)	It's not going to rain, . . . ?	. . .
b)	Yesterday was very cold, . . .?	. . .
c)	Last month was very wet, . . . ?	. . .
d)	It's really a fine day today, . . . ?	. . .

4. Bilde Minidialoge nach folgendem Muster!

| Is Peter a good boy? |
| No, he isn't, is he? |

a) Is Jane a good girl?
b) Was Peter in the garden?
c) Has Pat got a new bag?
d) Were the children at school?

Mrs Mags:	Oh, good morning, Mrs Dusty!	
Mrs Dusty:	Oh, Mrs Mags!	
	By the way, you ⎡like⎤ the Millers, ⎣don't⎦ you?	+ −
Mrs Mags:	No, I don't.	
	And you? You ⎡don't like⎤ them, ⎣do⎦ you?	− +
Mrs Dusty:	No, I don't like them, either!	
	The Millers aren't friendly.	
	Mrs Miller always ⎡wears⎤ fashionable clothes, ⎣doesn't⎦ she?	+ −
	You ⎡watched⎤ the Millers yesterday ⎣didn't⎦ you?	+ −
Mrs Mags:	Yes, I did.	
	You ⎡didn't see⎤ their new car, ⎣did⎦ you?	− +
Mrs Dusty:	...	

Beachte! „NICHT WAHR?" mit einem ⎡Hauptzeitwort im Vordersatz⎤ !

Vordersatz	positiv	negativ
Gegenwart	do.../ does...	don't.../ doesn`t...
Mitvergangenheit	did...	didn't...

angehängte Frage
(question-tag)

1. *Unterscheide „Gegenwart" – „Mitvergangenheit"!*
   Ergänze „NICHT WAHR?"!

a) Mrs Miller bought a car, . . . ?
b) Mr Miller comes home at 10, . . . ?
c) Mrs Miller buys everything in Regent Street, . . . ?
d) Mrs Miller wore a new fur-coat, . . . ?
e) Mr Miller runs a big shop, . . . ?
f) The Millers don't work in summer, . . . ?
g) Mrs Miller didn't help her husband, . . . ?

2. Bilde Dialoge!

A:

This These	shoes pullover pen books	belongs belong	to you,	doesn't it? don't they?

B:

Yes,	it does. they do.

3. Bilde Minidialoge nach folgendem Muster!

> Does Mr Miller write books?
> Yes, he does, doesn't he?

a) Does Mrs Miller do the shopping?
b) Does Mr Miller wash his car?
c) Does Mr Miller work in the garden?
d) Does Mrs Miller like swimming?

4. Bilde Minidialoge nach folgendem Muster!

> Do the Millers play tennis?
> No, they don't, do they?

a) Do the Millers travel to Austria in winter?
b) Do the Millers fly to Greece in summer?
c) Do the Millers go to the theatre?
d) Do the Millers watch TV?

WHY NOT? . . . BECAUSE . . .

Tom:	Hello, Mrs Brown! This is Tom speaking!
Mrs Brown:	Hello, Tom!
Tom:	I'd like to speak to Jim because I want to play football with him.
Mrs Brown:	Jim can't play football. He is in bed.
Tom:	Pardon - why not?
Mrs Brown:	He can't play football because he is ill.
Tom:	Is it possible to speak to Jim?
Mrs Brown:	I'm sorry! Jim can't get up. He is too weak.
Tom:	Pardon - why not?
Mrs Brown:	He can't get up because he is too weak.
Tom:	Oh, I'm sorry. Give my love to Jim! Good-bye, Mrs Brown!

Beachte!

BECAUSE (= weil) . . . leitet eine **Begründung** oder **Erklärung** ein.

Vor BECAUSE steht kein Beistrich!

1. Ergänze die passenden Begründungssätze!

Sue can't go to the cinema . . .
Jane wants to buy some presents . . .
Peter can't play in the garden . . .
Pat is late for school . . .

BECAUSE

↓

> . . . it's too cold today.
> . . . she's got to do her homework.
> . . . he missed the bus.
> . . . it's Christmas.

2. *Verbinde die beiden Sätze mit "because"! Überlege zuerst, welcher Satz der Begründungssatz ist!*

a) Tom would like to speak to Jim.
   He wants to play tennis with him.
b) He is too tired.
   He can't do his homework.
c) Ann wants to drink tea.
   She is thirsty.
d) Betty wants to eat an apple.
   She is hungry.
e) Granny can't play football.
   She is too old.

3. *Lies den Dialog gut durch, dann bilde weitere Begründungssätze!*

   Jim can't . . .

a) . . . play tennis / ill
b) . . . go to school / too weak
c) . . . play the piano / too busy
d) . . . sing a song / too hoarse
e) . . . do his homework / too tired

4. *Versuche ein ähnliches Gespräch wie im Kästchen zu Beginn des Kapitels!*

   Verwende die Angaben von Nr. 3!

5. *Finde eine „gute Ausrede"!*

a) I'm late for school because . . .
b) My copy-book is not in my satchel . . .
c) I didn't study the new words . . .
d) I didn't go to school . . .
e) I can't help you . . .

15 | DON'T BE SO NOSY!

Little Jack: Does Tom learn English?
Mummy: No, he doesn't.

Little Jack: Why doesn't he learn English?
Mummy: He doesn't learn English because he is too
           tired.

Little Jack: Mummy, do you like coffee?
Mummy: No, I don't.

Little Jack: Why don't you like coffee?
Mummy: I don't like coffee because it's too bitter.

Little Jack: Mummy, why . . .?
Mummy: Stop asking "why-questions"! Don't be so
           nosy!

1. Bilde Dialoge nach folgendem Muster!

Why can't Jim go out?
He can't go out **because** he has no umbrella.

a) Pat: not write a letter / no pen
b) Ann: not eat her breakfast / not hungry
c) Bert: not ask the teacher / afraid of him
d) Joe: not go to school / sore foot
e) Betty: not sing a song / a cold

2. Bilde Dialoge nach folgendem Muster!

Why does Jim not go out?
He doesn't go out **because** he has no umbrella.

Verwende die Angaben von Nr. 1!

48

3. Bilde Dialoge nach folgendem Muster!

> **Why** did Jim not go out?
> He didn't go out **because** he had no umbrella.

Verwende die Angaben von Nr. 1!

4. Ergänze die fehlenden Fragen!

a) Why . . . ? **Jim can't go to school** because he is ill.

b) Why . . . ? **Tom and Ann don't like tonic water** because it's too bitter.

c) Why . . . ? **Jack and Joe can't write their exercises** because they have no pen.

d) Why . . . ? **Peter didn't put on his pullover** because it was too hot.

e) Why . . . ? **Mary doesn't take off her coat because** it's too cold.

f) Why . . . ? **Joe didn't sing** because he was too hoarse.

g) Why . . . ? **Nelly doesn't do her exercises** because she is too lazy.

h) Why . . . ? **The children don't play in the garden** because it is very cold.

5. Versuche folgendes Gespräch auf Englisch!

Little Jack: fragt, ob Peter zu Hause sei
Mutter: verneint

Little Jack: fragt, warum Peter nicht zu Hause sei
Mutter: sagt, er sei nicht zu Hause, weil er schwimmen gegangen sei

16 | AT THE TRAVEL AGENCY

Clerk: Good afternoon!
Tom and Betty: We'd like to travel to London.
Clerk: Oh, what a good idea!

London sights are fascinating, its theatres and cinemas are thrilling, Madam Tussaud's is amusing! Oxford Street is exciting — London is interesting!

1. Lies den Dialog gut durch!
   Bilde fünf sinnvolle Sätze!

London		amusing.
London sights	is	thrilling.
London cinemas		exciting.
Madam Tussaud's	are	fascinating.
Oxford Street		interesting.

2. Bilde Dialoge nach folgendem Muster!

A: **Why** do Tom and Betty want to travel to London?
B: They want to travel to London **because** London sights are fascinating.

a) ... London theatres and cinemas / thrilling
b) ... Madam Tussaud's / amusing
c) ... Oxford Street / exciting
d) ... London / interesting

3. Bilde Sätze nach folgendem Muster!

London sights are fascinating - **so** the children want to travel to London.

Verwende die Angaben von Nr. 2!

4. Bilde Dialoge nach folgendem Muster!

A: Why do the children travel to London?
B: Well, London sights are fascinating!
   That's why the children travel to London.

Verwende die Angaben von Nr. 2!

5. Bilde Sätze nach folgendem Muster!

London buses are quick.
That's why many Londoners go by bus.

a) London taxis
b) The Underground
c) London railways
d) Green Line Buses

WHAT CAN WE PLAY THIS AFTERNOON?

a [ei]	
b [bi:]	
c [si:]	
d [di:]	
e [i:]	
f [ef]	
g [dʒi:]	
h [eitʃ]	
i [ai]	
j [dʒei]	
k [kei]	
l [el]	
m [em]	
n [en]	
o [əu]	
p [pi:]	
q [kju:]	
r [ɑ:]	
s [es]	
t [ti:]	
u [ju:]	
v [vi:]	
w [dʌblju:]	
x [eks]	
y [wai]	
z [zed]	

Tom: What can we play this afternoon?

Peter: I'd like to play chess.

Tom: What — jazz? You can't play the piano, you can't play the trumpet, you can't play, . . . Do you really want to play jazz?

Peter: Yes, of course, Tom!

Tom: We haven't got records and we haven't got a record-player — so it's impossible to play jazz.

Peter: But I want to play chess!

Mum: Stop quarrelling boys!
Peter, please spell the word "chess"!

Peter: [si: / eitʃ / i: / es / es]

Mum: Tom, please, spell the word "jazz"!

Tom: [dʒei / ei / zed / zed]

Mum: You see — chess and jazz — that's something different!

Tom: OK, Peter, let's play!
I'm very much looking forward to playing chess with you!

1. Lies den Dialog im Kästchen gut durch! Bilde „Minidialoge" nach folgendem Muster!

A: Do you really want to play tennis?
B: We haven't got a racket and we haven't got a ball - so it's impossible to play tennis!

a) go skiing / anorak, sticks
b) go swimming / swimming suit, bathing-cap
c) play cards / cards, money
d) play records / records, record-player

2. *Wo wohnt Jim?*

He lives in [en/ i: / dʌblju: / si: / ei / es / ti: / el / i:]

3. *Lies die Buchstaben auf dieser Schreibmaschine auf Englisch!*
   Vergleiche sie mit eurer Schreibmaschine zu Hause!

4. *Lies die internationalen Kraftfahrzeugkennzeichen auf*
   Englisch!

(A)   (GB)   (F)   (H)   (GR)   (S)   (TR)

5. *Ordne die Ländernamen den Kraftfahrzeugkennzeichen zu und*
   bilde Sätze!

(A) Austria   ( ) Turkey   ( ) Hungary   ( ) Sweden

( ) Great Britain   ( ) France   ( ) Greece

"A" stands for "Austria".

6. *Das englische Alphabet hilft dir beim Lesen folgender Abkür-*
   zungen. Was bedeuten sie? Ordne der Abkürzung die ent-
   sprechende Bedeutung zu!

1	USA		Television
2	SOS		United States of America
3	UK		Save Our Souls
4	BBC		Very Important Person
5	TV		United Kingdom
6	VIP		British Broadcasting Corporation

Reporter: Welcome to London, Miss Smily! I'd like to ask you some questions! Where did you start your career?

Miss Smily: In Texas.

Reporter: When did you go to New York?

Miss Smily: I moved to New York when I was four.

Reporter: Why did you become an actress?

Miss Smily: I liked films!

Reporter: What did you like best when you were a little girl?

Miss Smily: Oh, films and cinemas.

Reporter: . . . and my last question: Did you enjoy your flight?

Miss Smily: Oh yes, I did . . . and London is marvellous!

Beachte die Frage nach Ort, Zeit, Grund, . . . in der **Mitvergangenheit!**

Where .... ?
When .... ?
How long ..... ?   } gefolgt von **DID** + **Hauptzeitwort in der Nennform** (Infinitive)
Why .... ?
What .... ?

1. *Lies den Dialog im Kästchen gut durch! Beantworte folgende Fragen mit Kurzantworten!*

a) Did Miss Smily start her career in London?
b) Did she go to New York when she was five?
c) Did she like theatres best when she was a girl?
d) Did she enjoy her flight?

2. *Ergänze die Fragen zu folgendem Interview?*

Reporter: Where . . .
Miss Pinky: I went to school in London.
Reporter: When . . .
Miss Pinky: I wanted to become an actress when I was six.
Reporter: Why . . .
Miss Pinky: I wanted to become an actress because I liked films.

3. *Ein Reporter fragt Miss Fatty,*

a) wo sie zur Schule gegangen sei,
b) warum sie nach London gereist sei,
c) was ihr in London am besten gefallen habe,
d) wann sie nach London gekommen sei,
e) ob sie gestern angekommen sei.

4. *Bilde Fragesätze aus folgenden Bausteinen!*

a) Where | you | your | did | start | career ?
b) What | in | New | York | you | did | do ?
c) Why | become | you | an | actress | did ?
d) When | to | come | London | you | did ?

5. *Frage nach dem unterstrichenen Satzteil!*

a) Miss Smily lived in Texas.
b) She liked films best.
c) She came to New York in 1980.
d) She came to London because she wanted to see Piccadilly Circus.

CAN YOU TELL ME THE WAY TO . . . , PLEASE?

Tom: Can you tell me the way to Nelson's Column, please?

Policeman:
Cross Bedford Street.
Walk straight on as far as
St. Martin's Lane.
Turn left, walk straight on
as far as Trafalgar Square!

Tom: Thank you!

Beachte die Redewendungen!

cross . . . überqueren / straight on . . . gerade aus / as far as . . . bis zu / turn left (right) . . . nach links (rechts) abbiegen / take the second on the left . . . bei der zweiten Straße nach links abbiegen / take the third on the right . . . bei der dritten Straße nach rechts abbiegen / turn round . . . umkehren

---

1. *Die Kinder erkundigen sich nach dem Weg.*
   Bilde Sätze nach folgendem Muster!

---

a) Where is the museum, please?
b) Can you tell me the way to the museum, please?
c) Excuse me, can you tell me the way to the museum?

Verwende: cinema, park, theatre, restaurant, hospital, town hall, . . .

2. *Ein Tourist fragt den Polizisten nach dem Weg.*
   Der Polizist antwortet, er soll

a) geradeaus gehen,
b) die Park Street überqueren,

c) bis zur Verkehrsampel gehen (traffic-light)
d) den Zebrastreifen überqueren (zebra crossing)

3. *Ein Autofahrer erkundigt sich nach dem Weg.*
   Der Polizist sagt ihm, er soll

a) umkehren,
b) bei der zweiten Straße nach links abbiegen,
c) bei der dritten Straße nach rechts abbiegen,
d) bis zur Verkehrsampel fahren, dann nach rechts abbiegen,
e) bis zum Zebrastreifen fahren, dann nach links abbiegen.

4. *Die Kinder erkundigen sich nach folgenden Sehens-*
   würdigkeiten!

> Excuse me, can you tell me the way to Marble Arch, please?

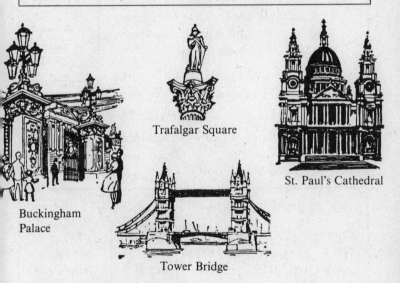

Trafalgar Square

St. Paul's Cathedral

Buckingham
Palace

Tower Bridge

5. *Lies den Dialog im Kästchen zu Beginn des Abschnitts noch*
   einmal durch!
   Versuche anhand des Planes ähnliche Gespräche mit deinem
   Partner!

a) mündlich   b) schriftlich

57

Ann: Good morning, Sue! Do you often go to school by Underground?

Sue: No, I don't. I usually go by bus. But this morning I got up too late, so I went by Underground — it's quicker!
And how about you, Ann?
Do you always go to school by bike?

Ann: Oh, no! I sometimes go by car. Dad takes me to school in his car. But today the weather is lovely, that's why I took my bike.

Sue: Look! Mr Green, our maths teacher! He always walks on foot, he never goes by tram or by bus.

Ann: Yes, walking is really the best thing to do — but Mr Green lives opposite our school!

BY

ON

Beachte die Stellung dieser Umstandswörter !

OFT	I	often	go ...
NIE	He has	never	got ...
GEWÖHNLICH ..	We	usually	write ...
MANCHMAL	She	sometimes	sings ...
IMMER	I	always	help ...

↓ ↑
VOR dem Haupt-
zeitwort

1. Beantworte folgende Fragen in vollständigen Sätzen!

a) Does Sue often go to school by Underground?
b) Does Sue usually go by bus?
c) Does Ann always go by bike?
d) Does Ann sometimes go by car?
e) Does Mr Green always go by Underground?
f) What does Mr Green always do?
g) What about you?

2. Setze das Umstandswort an die richtige Stelle im Satz!

a) I go to school by bike. (gewöhnlich)
b) The Millers travel to England in summer. (oft)
c) Pat does his work in the afternoon. (immer)
d) I have got a lot of homework. (immer)
e) I play tennis in the afternoon. (manchmal)

3. Versuche Dialoge nach folgendem Muster!

> A: How does Mr Miller usually get to his office?
>   By bus?
> B: No, he always gets to his office by car.

a) Mrs Brown . . . shop . . . train / tram
b) The Coopers . . . to Greece . . . car / plane
c) Mr White . . . to the mountains . . . bus / helicopter
d) The Millers . . . to Italy . . . train / plane

4. Versuche folgendes Gespräch auf Englisch!

A: fragt, ob Tom immer mit dem Fahrrad fährt
B: verneint und sagt, er gehe gewöhnlich zu Fuß, manchmal fahre er mit der Untergrundbahn.

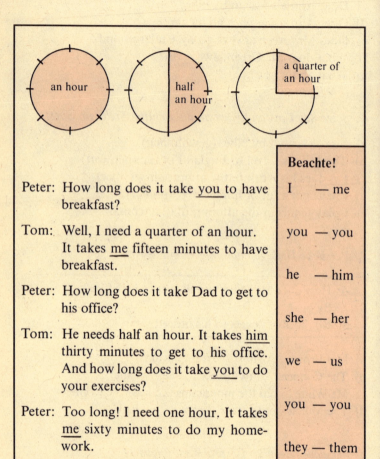

an hour	
half an hour	
a quarter of an hour	

Beachte!

Peter: How long does it take <u>you</u> to have breakfast?

Tom: Well, I need a quarter of an hour. It takes <u>me</u> fifteen minutes to have breakfast.

Peter: How long does it take Dad to get to his office?

Tom: He needs half an hour. It takes <u>him</u> thirty minutes to get to his office. And how long does it take <u>you</u> to do your exercises?

Peter: Too long! I need one hour. It takes <u>me</u> sixty minutes to do my home-work.

I	—	me
you	—	you
he	—	him
she	—	her
we	—	us
you	—	you
they	—	them

Beachte!

BRAUCHEN

I need
. . . allgemein

it takes me
. . . auf Zeitdauer bezogen

1. *Lies das Gespräch im Kästchen gut durch!*
   Beachte jeweils den Ausdruck für „brauchen"!

2. *Beantworte folgende Fragen!*

a) How long does it take you to go to school?
b) How long does it take your mother to prepare dinner?
c) How long does it take your boy friend to study English?
d) How long does it take your friends to do their homework?
e) How long does it take you and your friend to write a test?

3. *Bilde Dialoge nach folgendem Muster!*

> A: How long did it take the Millers to fly to Italy?
> B: It took them four hours to fly to Italy.

a) Tom: to travel to London . . . two hours
b) Ann: to water the flowers . . . five minutes
c) The Coopers: to dig the garden . . . three hours
d) The Smiths: to paint the house . . . one day

4. *Bilde Dialoge nach folgendem Muster!*

> A: Excuse me, sir, how long does it take me to get to
>   Marble Arch?
> B: Go by bus! Then it takes you five minutes!

a) Buckingham Palace / by bus / ten minutes
b) Trafalgar Square / by Underground / five minutes
c) Tower Bridge / by boat / twenty minutes
d) St. Paul's Cathedral / by bus / three minutes

5. *Frage deinen Freund, wie lange er für*

a) seine Hausübung braucht,
b) seinen Schulweg braucht,
c) sein Frühstück braucht.

TRY THIS TEST   UNIT 9 - 21

A. *Streiche den Buchstaben v o r dem Wort durch, das in die Lücke paßt!*

> Last winter Joe . . . skiing.
> a) go   b) goes   c) to go   ~~d)~~ went

1. I . . . my holidays in London.
   a) to spend   b) spend   c) spent   d) spends

2. Tom . . . in Italy last summer.
   a) were   b) is   c) to be   d) was

3. Did you see Rome? Yes, we . . . in Rome, too.
   a) were   b) is   c) to be   d) was

4. What . . . the weather like yesterday?
   a) were   b) is   c) to be   d) was

5. Where did you . . . your holidays?
   a) to spend   b) spend   c) spent   d) spends

6. It was fine, so I . . . swimming.
   a) to go   b) goes   c) went   d) go

7. We travelled to London and . . . Big Ben.
   a) see   b) saw   c) to see   d) sees

8. The children . . . at school.
   a) were   b) was   c) is   d) to be

9. Last week Sue . . . in London.
   a) to arrive   b) arrives   c) arrived   d) arrive

10. Joe . . . in the country last month.
    a) stay   b) stayed   c) to stay   d) stays

11. Yesterday Ann . . . tennis.
    a) plays   b) play   c) to play   d) played

12. Did you . . . London?
    a) liked   b) likes   c) to like   d) like

points: 12

B. *Ergänze jeweils die Verneinung!*

> Pat wrote a letter but I *didn't write* a letter.

1. Ann went swimming but Nelly . . . swimming.
2. Sue plays tennis but Jack . . . tennis.
3. The children like ice-cream but they . . . spinach.
4. Joe asked the teacher but Pat . . . him.
5. Jack saw Tower Bridge but Joe . . . Tower Bridge.
6. Susan reads books but Nelly . . . books.
7. We like coffee but we . . . wine.
8. He took a photo of Big Ben but he . . . a photo of St. Paul's.

points: 8

C. *Ergänze jeweils „ . . . . , nicht wahr?"!*

> Joe likes tea, **doesn't he?**

1. Pat can't sing, . . . ?
2. Ann was in the garden, . . . ?
3. The children wrote 6 letters, . . . ?
4. They didn't read this book, . . . ?
5. Jack plays the piano, . . . ?
6. Nelly and Joe sing English songs, . . . ?   points: 6

D. *Frage nach dem unterstrichenen Satzteil!*

> Joe came home at six. **When did he come home?**

1. Pat read a book.. . .
2. Ann arrived at four. . . .
3. The children played in the park. . . .
4. She came to London because she wanted to see Big Ben. . . .

points: 4

E. *Das folgende Gespräch soll nur sinngemäß wiedergegeben werden! . . .*

Erkundige dich nach dem Weg zur Tower Bridge.	**Can you tell me the way to Tower Bridge?**
Geh geradeaus bis zur Verkehrsampel.	
Wie lange brauche ich zur Tower Bridge?	
Fahr mit dem Bus, dann brauchst du 5 Minuten zur Tower Bridge.	
Bedanke dich.	

points: 8

F. *Numeriere die folgenden Satzbausteine so, daß ein richtiger Satz entsteht!*

I	by bike	usually	to school	go
1	5	2	4	3

1. Tom   sometimes   in the garden   plays
2. We   to London   by car   go   often
3. do   I   always   my   exercises   in the morning
4. always   tennis   play   I   in the afternoon   points: 4

A. - F.: 42

Auswertung des Tests siehe Seite 35.

63

AS COLD AS . . . AS HOT AS . . .
AS WARM AS . . .

Tom: It's cool in London, isn't it?
What do you think? Is it cool in Vienna, too?

Ann: Let's have a look into the newspaper!

Tom: Oh, in Vienna it's just
as cold as in London!
And what about Cambridge?

Ann: In Cambridge it's just
as cold as in London.

Tom: Let's travel to Cairo!

Cairo	
Cambridge	20°
London	8°
Madrid	8°
Vienna	12°
	8°

Beachte!

Gleichheit wird ausgedrückt!

AS	adjective	AS
↓		↓
SO	Eigenschaftswort	WIE

1. *Lies den Dialog im Kästchen gut durch!*
   Bilde ähnliche Dialoge zu folgenden Angaben!

a) Copenhagen ...... 2°   b) Vienna .... 20°
   Moscow .... 2°   Berlin .... 20°
   Oslo .... 2°   Paris .... 20°

c) Athens .... 32°
   Rome .... 32°
   Madrid .... 32°

2. *Welches Hauptwort paßt jeweils zum numerierten Eigen-*
   schaftswort?

1 hot	☐ the wind	7 blue	☐ stone
2 dark	☐ fire	8 hard	☐ ice
3 old	☐ the sun	9 cold	☐ the sky
4 white	☐ the night	10 bitter	☐ diamonds
5 bright	☐ snow	11 sharp	☐ a knife
6 strong	☐ Rome	12 prescious	☐ coffee

3. *Treffende Vergleiche! Bilde Vergleiche mit den Wörtern von*
   Nr. 2!

```
as hot as fire, as dark as . . .
```

4. *Ergänze jeweils die vollständige Antwort!*

a) Is a boy as big as a man? No, . . .
b) Is a house as high as a mountain?
c) Is water as cold as ice?
d) Is beer as strong as wine?
e) Is the English test as difficult as the maths test?
f) Is Tom as old as his father?

5. *Vergleiche folgende Gegenstände!*

```
A: This pen is long. This pencil is long, too.
B: Look! The pencil is just as long as the pen.
```

a) exercise / test (difficult)
b) house / tree (high)
c) dress / suit (expensive)
d) Mary / Susan (beautiful)
e) gin / rum (strong)
f) Mr Miller / Mrs Miller (old)
g) tea / coffee (hot)
h) London / Rome (interesting)

23 | WINDOW-SHOPPING

Betty: I'm looking for a new skirt.

Ann: Look! There are three skirts in that shop-window!

cheap   cheaper   cheapest

Betty: Oh, yes, the red skirt is cheap .

Ann: And look! The green skirt is even cheaper .
... and the blue skirt is the cheapest .

Beachte die Steigerung des Eigenschaftsworts !

— Ein- und zweisilbige Eigenschaftswörter bilden die Steigerung mit **-er, -est**

long	- longer	- longest
big	- bigger	- biggest
happy	- happier	- happiest

— Dreisilbige Eigenschaftswörter bilden die Steigerung mit **more, most**

beautiful - **more** beautiful - **most** beautiful

1. Steigere folgende Eigenschaftswörter!

a) long
b) strong
c) short
d) high
e) happy
f) funny
g) sunny
h) heavy
i) interesting
j) expensive
k) beautiful
l) wonderful

2. Bilde Sätze nach folgendem Muster!

> Beer is strong.
> Wine is stronger.
> Whisky is strongest.

a) big: pig, cow, elephant
b) beautiful: Mary, Ann, Nelly
c) heavy: handbag, rucksack, suitcase
d) expensive: Mini, Jaguar, Rolls Royce
e) easy: English test, French test, maths test
f) interesting: London, Vienna, Rome

3. Lies den Dialog im Kästchen noch einmal gut durch, dann versuche ähnliche Gespräche!

a) cheap: blue jacket / white / red
b) nice: green dress / red / white
c) expensive: brown coat / black / red
d) beautiful: pink pullover / blue / grey

4. Bilde möglichst viele sinnvolle Fragen und beantworte sie!

Is it	cheaper more expensive	to eat to drink	wine fish bread Cola	or	whisky? steaks? sandwiches? water?

Mrs Brown: Good morning, Mrs White!
Lovely day today, isn't it?

Mrs White: Yes, very nice indeed - bright and sunny!
Yesterday it was worse . There was less
sunshine.

Mrs Brown: It can't be better .
But the weather forecast is bad . . .

Mrs White: The weathermen are always wrong, aren't
they? I know more about the weather
than they do.

Mrs Brown: Yes, of course! But look at those black
clouds . . .

Beachte die unregelmäßige Steigerung des
Eigenschaftswortes!

good	- **better**	- **best**
bad	- **worse**	- **worst**
much (viel)	- **more**	- **most**
little (wenig)	- **less**	- **least**

1. Lies den Text im Kästchen sorgfältig durch!
Was bedeuten folgende Steigerungsformen im Deutschen?

worse: . . .   less: . . .   better: . . .   more: . . .

*2. Welche der folgenden Sätze stimmen sinngemäß mit dem Text
überein?*

	yes	no
Rainy day today, isn't it?	☐	☒

a) Not very nice today!
b) Yesterday it was worse.
c) Yesterday it was sunnier.
d) There was more sunshine.
e) The weathermen are always right.
f) Mrs White knows more about the
   weather than the weathermen.
g) There are no black clouds in the sky.

3. Bilde Sätze nach folgendem Muster!

> Today the weather is bad.
> Yesterday it was even worse.

a) Today's dinner was bad.
b) Today's TV programme is bad.
c) Today's football match was bad.
d) Today's news are very bad.

4. Bilde möglichst viele sinnvolle Sätze!

It's better	to eat to drink	less more	chocolate. wine. black coffee. milk. juice. vegetables.

5. Beantworte die Fragen nach folgendem Muster!

> When it is cold it's the best thing to put on warm boots.

What's the best thing to do . . .

a) . . . when it is hot?
b) . . . when you are hungry?
c) . . . when you are tired?
d) . . . when you are thirsty?

I AM STRONGER THAN YOU!

Tom: I'm stronger than you!

Peter: No, you are not! I am stronger than you!

Father: Don't quarrel!
         Tom is just as strong as Peter!

Tom: I'm taller than you!

Peter: No, you are not! I am taller than you!

Father: Don't quarrel!
         Tom is just as tall as Peter!

Beachte!

Ungleichheit wird ausgedrückt!

stronger	THAN	stärker ALS
more beautiful	THAN	schöner ALS
better	THAN	besser ALS

↓

2. Form des
Eigenschafts-   + THAN ..... drückt **Ungleichheit /**
wortes   **Verschiedenheit** aus

*1. Lies den Dialog im Kästchen gut durch, dann versuche ähnliche
   Gespräche!*

a) Ann, Betty, Mother: beautiful
b) Peter, Jim, Father: clever
c) Jane, Susan, Mother: intelligent
d) Pat, Joe, Father: quick

2. Bilde Sätze nach folgendem Muster!

Wine is stronger **than** beer.
Whisky is stronger **than** wine.

a) beautiful: Mary, Ann, Nelly
b) big: pig, cow, elephant
c) heavy: handbag, rucksack, suitcase
d) expensive: Mini, Jaguar, Rolls Royce
e) easy: English test, French test, maths test

3. *„Wärmer" oder „kälter"?*
   Vergleiche die Temperaturen
   folgender Städte!

TEMPERATURES	C	F
Athens fair	11	(52)
Bangkok sun	33	(91)
Barbados cloud	29	(84)
Barcelona sun	15	(59)
Berlin cloud	3	(37)
Birmingham cloud	12	(54)
Bristol cloud	13	(55)
Brussels sun	10	(50)
Cardiff sun	12	(54)
Dublin sun	11	(52)
Gibraltar cloud	16	(61)
Hong Kong sun	23	(73)
Honolulu cloud	29	(84)
Las Palmas sun	21	(70)
Lisbon rain	14	(57)
London rain	11	(52)
Los Angeles rain	19	(66)
Madrid cloud	9	(48)
Malaga cloud	17	(63)
Malta fair	18	(64)
Miami cloud	26	(79)
Moscow cloud	-3	(27)
New York sun	6	(43)
Nice sun	17	(63)
Paris sun	11	(52)
Rome sun	18	(64)
Sydney cloud	23	(73)
Tel Aviv cloud	18	(64)

Yesterday it was
warmer in Athens **than**
in Berlin.

a) Athens - Bangkok
b) Birmingham - Bristol
c) Gibraltar - London
d) Miami - Moscow
e) Rome - Paris
f) Sydney - Tel Aviv

4. *Stelle folgende Sätze richtig!*

Pat is older **than** his father.
No, Pat isn't older **than** his father.
Father is older **than** Pat.

a) A house is higher **than** a mountain.
b) A chair is **more** comfortable than a bed.
c) Boys are **better** pupils **than** girls.
d) A village is larger **than** a town.
e) A bicycle is faster **than** a car.
f) Beer is stronger **than** whisky.
g) A handbag is bigger **than** a suitcase.
h) A Rolls Royce is cheaper **than** a Mini.
i) A pig is bigger **than** an elephant.

71

Sunny spells, risk of showers.
Outlook: Bright spells, with showers.

1, 2, 3: Rain at first, becoming dry. Max 9C (48F).

4, 5, 6, 7, 8, 9, 10, 15: Mostly dry, sunny spells. Max 9C (48F).

11, 12, 13, 14, 20, 21, 22, 25, 26, 29: Sunny spells, scattered showers. Max 8C (46F).

16, 17, 18, 19, 23, 24, 27, 28: Mostly dry. Max 8C (46F).

Sun sets 3.52 p.m., rises 7.51 a.m. tomorrow. Moon rises 2.43 p.m., sets 6.50 a.m. tomorrow. London Lighting-up time: 4.23 p.m. to 7.22 a.m. tomorrow. High water at London Bridge: 12.27 p.m. and 12.52 a.m. tomorrow.

TWENTY-FOUR HOURS TO 6 P.M. YESTERDAY. — Warmest place in Britain: Exeter 14C (57F). Coldest: Stornoway (O. Hebrides) 2C (36F). Sunniest: Newquay (Cornwall) 4.1 hrs. Wettest: Machrihanish (Kintyre) 0.95 ins.

Beachte das Vokabular!
sunny spells . . . sonnige Abschnitte / showers . . . Schauer / sun sets . . . die Sonne geht unter / sun rises . . . die Sonne geht auf / moon . . . Mond

1. Lies die Wettervorhersage gut durch! Stelle fest, ob folgende Sätze mit dem Wetterbericht übereinstimmen oder nicht!

	yes	no
Sunny spells, risk of showers.	☒	☐

a) Bright spells, no showers.
b) District 1, 2, 3: Rain at first.
c) District 28: mostly dry.
d) Sun sets 4.52 p.m.
e) Sun rises 7.51 a.m.
f) Warmest place in Britain yesterday:
   London
g) Coldest place yesterday: Bristol.
h) Sunniest place: Newquay.

2. Beantworte anhand des Zeitungsausschnitts folgende Fragen!

a) Is the weather forecast very bad?
b) Do the weathermen say "RAIN"?
c) What can you say about the temperature in London?
d) What can you say about the temperature on the
   Shetland Islands?
e) What was the warmest place in Britain?
f) Where was it coldest?
g) Was it sunniest in Newquay?
h) Write down the name of the wettest place!

3. Bilde Sätze nach folgenden Mustern!

> It's **as warm** in London **as** in Exeter.
> It's warm**er** in London **than** in Manchester.

Benütze die Angaben im obersten Kästchen und vergleiche:

a) London - Aberdeen   c) Belfast   - Bristol
b) Cardiff - Edinburgh   d) Newcastle - Glasgow

4. Beachte die Uhrzeit!

> The sun sets at eight minutes to four.

a) The sun rises: 7.51   b) The moon rises: 2.43
          c) The moon sets: 6.50

THE FORTUNE-TELLER
WILL TELL YOU THE FUTURE

Mary: Did you meet my great-grandmother yesterday?
Sue: No, I didn't.
Mary: It's a pity! She reads people's hands and she will read your hands, too.
Sue: Oh, that's funny! Let's visit her!

Fortune-teller: . . .your hand tells me:

You	will be	very rich.
You	will live	in America.
You	will marry	a young man.
You	will become	President of the USA.

Sue: Shall I be happy?
Fortune-teller:
      No, you will not be happy!

Beachte die Zukunft (Future Tense) !

I	**shall** get . . .	Das gesprochene Englisch
You	will get . . .	verwendet jeweils die
He / She	will get . . .	**Kurzform → I'll, you'll . . .**
We	**shall** get . . .	**we'll, they'll.** Daher wird
You	will get . . .	nicht zwischen "shall" und
They	will get . . .	„will" unterschieden.

Verneinung:

| I | shall not get . . . | = I | shan't get . . . |
| You | will not get . . . | = You | won't get . . . |

1. *Lies den Dialog gut durch! Beachte die Sätze in der Zukunft!*
   Was könnte die Wahrsagerin noch gesagt haben?

Verwende: live for a long time
have 10 children
get a good job
live in Washington
become a grandmother

2. Was die Kinder fürs neue Jahr versprechen:

We'll clean our teeth.

Verwende: be punctual, get up early, go to bed in time, help in
the kitchen, wash our necks, do our homework, . . .

3. Bilde möglichst viele Sätze!

			go swimming.
Next summer	I	shall	travel to New York.
Tomorrow	Tom	will	go sightseeing in London.
			play tennis.

4. Bilde möglichst viele Sätze!

		go to school	
Peter	shan't	go skiing	tomorrow.
I	won't	go skating	next year.

*5. Wie **wird** das Wetter **sein?** Ergänze die Lücken!*

It . . . fine tomorrow. There . . . no clouds in the sky.
It . . . warm and sunny. It . . . warmer than today.
It . . . a fine day.

6. Ergänze „ – nicht wahr?"!

a) Tom will travel to England, . . . ?
b) I shan't play tennis, . . . ?
c) Jim won't ask the teacher, . . . ?
d) Peter will help us, . . . ?
e) We shall bake a cake, . . . ?
f) Nelly won't read this book, . . . ?

Mrs Brown and Mrs White **want** to buy some presents, so they enter a department store.

Department Guide	
fourth floor	Cafeteria
third floor	Furniture / Carpets / Curtains
second floor	Men's Wear / Sports Equipment
first floor	Ladies' Wear / Children's Wear
ground floor	Toilet Articles / Music / Photography
basement	Restaurant / Supermarket

Mrs Brown: Little Tommy **wants** a pair of skis, so I'll buy a pair of skis for him. **He'll** be glad to get new skis.

Mrs White: Little Sue **wants** some records and a pullover, so **I'll** buy records and a pullover for her. **She'll** be happy to get some records. And what **will** y o u buy for your friends.

Beachte!

Tommy **wants** . . .   he **will** be glad . . .
              ↓   ↓
       er möchte (er will)   er wird . . . (ZUKUNFT)

1. Beantworte folgende Fragen!

a) Why do Mrs Brown and Mrs White go to a department store?
b) Who will buy a pair of skis?
c) Who will buy some records?
d) Where will Mrs Brown buy skis?
e) Where will Mrs Brown buy some records?

2. Ordne die Waren den entsprechenden Abteilungen zu!

3	FURNITURE	skis	table	skirt
2	SPORTS	pullover	skateboard	shelf
	EQUIPMENT	soap	dress	coat
1	LADIES' WEAR	sugar	lipstick	skates
G	TOILET ARTICLES	comb	flour	cocoa
B	SUPERMARKET	chair	sideboard	blouse
		football	chocolate	tooth-brush

3. Bilde Sätze nach folgendem Muster!

Mrs Brown will buy skis.
She'll buy them on the second floor.
Mrs White will buy a pullover.
She'll buy it on the first floor.

Verwende die Wörter von Nr. 2!

4. Bilde Sätze nach folgendem Muster!

I want a blouse for my birthday.
I hope I'll get a blouse.

Verwende: skirt, pullover, shoes, dress, boots, . . .

5. Bilde mündlich einen Kettensatz, indem du den Satz jeweils um ein Wort verlängerst!

I'll go to a department store and I'll buy skis.
I'll go to a department store and I'll buy skis and a pullover.

CLEARANCE SALES!
EVERYTHING'S REDUCED!

Mrs Brown: What will you do tomorrow?

Mrs White: I'll go to town to get some stools and a chair bed and . . . Just look at this advertisement - there's a sale on! I'm afraid the day after tomorrow everything will be sold out.

Mrs Brown: I'll come with you! See you tomorrow!

£16 OFF

From our fashionable range of folding chairs MANY HALF PRICE OR LESS!

LAST CHANCE

Fold-away Chair
Red plastic seat and back

ALFA
♥ Previous Price £19.99
CLEARANCE PRICE **£3·99**

£10 OFF

LAST CHANCE

Bar Stool
Dark stained 27" high stool with elegantly carved legs.
COLONIAL
♣ Previous Price £14.99
CLEARANCE PRICE

SOLID PINE

£4·99

£30 OFF

Chair Bed
It's a prettily patterned chair.
It's a bed. At this price, it's a giveaway!

CHAIR BED
♥ Previous Price £49.99

LAST CHANCE

CLEARANCE PRICE **£19·99**

1. Beantworte folgende Fragen!

a) What will Mrs Brown do tomorrow?
b) What will Mrs White buy?
c) Is there a sale on?
d) Is there a chair bed on sale?
e) Why will Mrs White go to town tomorrow?
f) Who will come with her?

2. Bilde Sätze nach folgendem Muster!

> Mrs White says, "Look at this chair bed! It's previous price was £ 49.99. I'll get it for £ 19.99. £ 30 are off!"

Verwende die Angaben im Kästchen zu Beginn des Kapitels!

3. Übernimm die Rolle des Verkäufers!

Mrs White: Good afternoon! Can you show me the chair bed for £ 19.99, please?

Shop-assistant: Oh, it's a prettily . . . It's a . . . At this price. . .

Mrs White: And what about your fold-away chairs?

Shop-assistant: They're very cheap, only . . .

Mrs White: Are the seats made of leather?

Shop-assistant: No, it's a . . .

Mrs White: I'd like to have a look at the bar stools, too!

Shop-assistant: Just look at this . . .It's legs are . . .

Mrs White: I'll take one chair bed, four fold-away chairs and three bar stools.

Shop-assistant: That'll be . . . altogether.

79

Mrs Brown: Hello, Mrs White! Shopping in the Burlington Arcades?

Mrs White: Yes, I'm after some fine knitwear and some fine leather goods. I'm sure I'll find something beautiful in one of the 38 shops!

Mrs Brown: Just look at this beautiful │ **pullover** │!

Mrs White: The red │ one │ is very nice, but the green │ one │ is too expensive for me!

Mrs Brown: Look at these elegant **handbags!**

Mrs White: The black │ ones │ are really very nice, the brown │ ones │ are lovely, indeed — but too expensive altogether!

Mrs Brown: I think we'd rather go to a department store!

Beachte!

Um eine **Wiederholung des Hauptwortes** zu vermeiden, kann das │ Stützwort (PROP WORD) ONE │ gesetzt werden.

Look at this red pullover!
    Yes, the red │ ONE │ is really very nice!
Look at these red **pullovers!**
    Yes, the red │ ONES │ are really very nice!

1. *Lies den Dialog im Kästchen gut durch!*
    Beachte das Stützwort ONE!

2. *Bilde Dialoge nach folgendem Muster!*

> A: Tommy wants a black jacket. - And Sue?
> B: She wants a white one.

a) Mr Miller has a new house. - And Mr Johnson? (old)
b) Betty likes her long coat. - And Nelly? (short)
c) Mrs White bought an expensive handbag. -
    And Mrs Brown? (cheap)
d) John got a bad mark. - And Tom? (good)
e) Mary wrote a long letter. - And Peter? (short)

3. *Bilde Dialoge nach folgendem Muster!*

> A: Look at these nice **shirts**!
> B: The red **one** is lovely, but the black **ones** are old-fashioned.

a) blouses:
      green (beautiful)
      blue (too expensive)

b) cardigans:
      brown (rather cheap)
      black (really lovely)

c) dresses:
      white (beautiful)
      red (old-fashioned)

d) coats:
      blue (fashionable)
      red (too elegant)

4. *Versuche einen ähnlichen Dialog wie jenen im Kästchen!*

Verwende: after some handmade toys and a fine purse ... lovely doll ... big one ... nice ... small one ... too expensive ... purses ... green ones ... too small ... brown ones ... lovely

Last week the children visited their Granny in a little village near London. Granny asked them to do the shopping.

Granny: Children, there's no supermarket in our village! You've got to go to many different shops . . . Get me <u>some</u> jam, mustard, juice, . . . but don't buy <u>any</u> other things!

Where to buy these things:

AT THE

baker's
grocer's
green-grocer's
tobacco-nist's
butcher's

Shopping List

2 glasses of jam
2 bottles of juice
carrots
a box of sugar
2 jars of mustard
4 buns
2 loaves of bread

a piece of sausage
half a pound of beef
2 packets of sweets
2 bars of chocolate
2 packets of cigarettes

Beachte!

SOME
ANY
bedeutet

„etwas": some **jam**, . . . any **wool**, . .
in Verbindung mit der **Einzahl**

„einige": some **apples**, . . . any **boxes**
in Verbindung mit der **Mehrzahl**

Have you got ANY jam? No, we haven't ANY!	ANY: in Fragesätzen verneinten Sätzen
I want SOME jam! Here is SOME jam!	SOME: in positiven Sätzen

1. *Lies die Einkaufsliste gut durch und ordne die angegebenen Artikel den entsprechenden Geschäften zu!*

2. *Bilde Sätze nach folgendem Muster!*

> Can you tell us the way to the baker's, please?
> We've got to buy 2 loaves of bread.

a) to the grocer's b) to the greengrocer's c) to the tobacconist's

3. *Bilde Dialoge nach folgendem Muster!*

> A: Have you got **any** jam?
> B: Yes, we've got **some**.
> A: Then give me two glasses of jam, please.

Verwende: juice, bread, sweets, chocolate

4. *Bilde Minidialoge nach folgendem Muster!*

> A: Have you got **any** mustard?
> B: Oh, I'm sorry, there isn't **any** mustard left.

Verwende: sausage, beef, sugar, bread, juice

5. *Bilde Fragesätze nach folgenden Mustern und beantworte sie!*

> a) Did you buy **any** jam? - Yes, we bought **some** jam.
> b) Did you buy **any** sausage? -
>   No, we didn't buy **any** sausage.

Verwende: a) juice, bread, chocolate b) beef, sugar, mustard

6. *Bilde Minidialoge nach folgendem Muster!*

> A: **Two glasses of jam,** please!
> B: I'm sorry, there's only **one glass of jam** left!

Verwende: two jars of mustard, two bottles of juice, two loaves of bread, two packets of sweets, two bars of chocolate, . . .

Little Tommy: Tell me, Mum, what has a baker got to do?

Mum: A baker has got to bake bread.
A <u>baker</u> is a <u>person</u> who bakes bread.

Little Tommy: And Mum, what is this typewriter for?

Mum: A <u>typewriter</u> is a <u>thing</u> which we use for writing letters.

Little Tommy: And what about this computer?

Mum: A <u>computer</u> is a <u>thing</u> which we need for . . . Oh, Tommy, don't always ask silly questions!

Beachte die bezüglichen Fürwörter !

. . . a person ← who

. . . a thing ← which

auf Personen bezogen
(das Mädchen, welches . . .
der Mann, welcher . . .)

auf Dinge bezogen
(der Mantel, welcher . . .
das Buch, welches . . .)

1. "Who" oder "which"? Setze ein!

a) It was Betty . . . made the beds.
b) A pen is a thing . . . we need for writing.
c) It was Jane . . . wrote the exercise.
d) It was Joe . . . broke the glasses.
e) I don't like books . . . are boring.
f) Tom saw a film . . . was interesting.
g) This is the coat . . . was very expensive.
h) It was Nelly . . . fell asleep.

2. Welche Tätigkeit paßt zu welchem Beruf? Ordne die entsprechenden Zahlen zu!

1	baker		teach children
2	bus driver		steer jet planes
3	butcher		type letters
4	dentist		sell fine dresses
5	farmer		serve people
6	grocer		set people's hair
7	hairdresser		sell sugar and flour
8	pilot		milk the cows
9	secretary		repair teeth
10	shop-assistant		make sausages
11	teacher		drive buses
12	waiter		bake bread

3. Bilde Dialoge nach folgendem Muster!

> A: Is a baker **a person who** teaches children?
> B: No, a baker is **a person who** bakes bread.

Verwende die Angaben von Nr. 2!

4. Bilde Sätze nach folgendem Muster!

> I like interesting films.
> I like **films which** are interesting.

a) Peter doesn't read boring books.
b) The cat doesn't drink warm milk.
c) Betty can't answer difficult questions.
d) Joe likes easy tests.
e) Jane prefers difficult puzzles.

5. Verbinde jeweils 2 Sätze mit "who" oder "which"!

a) He took my book. It was on the table.
b) Here is the boy. He wants to help you.
c) Here is the man. He followed me.
d) This is Pat's brother. He lives in New York.
e) We'll take the train. It arrives in Brighton at 10.30.

Shop-assistant:	What can I do for you?
Mrs White:	I'd like a coat.
Shop-assistant:	We've got very nice coats. What size would you like?
Mrs White:	Size 38 will be all right.
Shop-assistant:	How do you like this green one?
Mrs White:	Oh, I think, it doesn't suit me.
Shop-assistant:	We've got a very nice red coat.
Mrs White:	It's really lovely! I'll try it on . . . This red coat doesn't fit.
Shop-assistant:	How about this blue coat? It's very fashionable.
Mrs White:	How much is it, please?
Shop-assistant:	Let me see - 82 £!
Mrs White:	I'll try it on . . . This blue coat suits me, it fits, but it doesn't go with my boots and my hat!
Shop-assistant:	I'm sorry, I can't help you but we're going to have some more coats in!

Beachte!

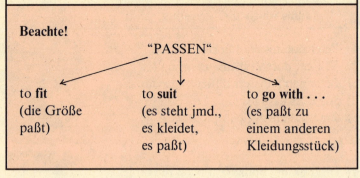

"PASSEN"

to **fit**	to **suit**	to **go with** . . .
(die Größe paßt)	(es steht jmd., es kleidet, es paßt)	(es paßt zu einem anderen Kleidungsstück)

1. Lies das Einkaufsgespräch im Kästchen gut durch und beachte, wie im Englischen das deutsche Wort "passen" ausgedrückt wird.

2. Bilde Minidialoge nach folgendem Muster!

> A: How do you like this green coat?
> B: Oh, I think, it doesn't suit me.

Verwende: black hat, blue dress, white skirt, red pullover, . . .

3. Bilde Dialoge nach folgendem Muster!

> A: This red dress doesn't fit. It's too wide!
> B: That doesn't matter! We can make it tighter!

Verwende: green skirt / too long / shorter
black jacket / too tight / wider
red costume / too short / longer
white frock / too big / smaller

4. Beachte die Einzahl bzw. Mehrzahl!

> This green skirt suits me, it fits, but it doesn't go with my pullover and my shoes.
>
> These blue trousers suit me, they fit, but they don't go with my pullover and my shoes.

Verwende: black hat, red cap, green shorts, white socks, . . .

5. Beantworte die Fragen nach folgendem Muster!

> A: Does this pullover fit?
> B: Yes, that's the pullover which fits.

a) Does this skirt fit?
b) Does this blouse fit?
c) Does this dress fit?
d) Does this hat fit?
e) Does this cap fit?

6. Versuche mit deinem Partner ein ähnliches Gespräch wie jenes im Kästchen!

87

34 WHAT WAS GOING ON WHEN . . . ?

Yesterday the children were very naughty in class. When Mrs Smith, the English teacher, came into the classroom . . .

> . . . Tom was sitting on the cupboard,
> . . . Betty was standing on the table,
> . . . Ann was sitting in the wastepaper-basket,
> . . . Jim and Joe were playing football, . . .

When the lesson was over Mrs Smith told Mrs White: "Such a naughty class!

> While Tom was sitting on the cupboard,
> Betty was standing on the table.
>
> While Betty was standing on the table,
> Ann was sitting in the wastepaper-basket.
>
> While Ann was sitting in the wastepaper-basket,
> Jim and Joe were playing football."

Beachte die Dauerform der Mitvergangenheit !

When Mrs Smith **came** into the classroom, (kurze Handlung)

Jim and Joe were playing football. (lange Handlung)

Ann was sitting in the wastepaper-basket, while . . .

Betty was standing on the table.

Zwei Handlungen laufen parallel nebeneinander.

1. *Welcher Satz stellt die längere, bzw. kürzere Handlung dar? Bilde Sätze!*

> Mum / read a book - Dad / come home
> Mum **was reading** a book when Dad **came** home.

a) Peter / enter the classroom - teacher / sing a song
b) Ann / do her exercise - Mum / enter her room
c) Dad / read the newspaper - telephone / ring
d) Sue / play on the piano - Dad / open the door

2. *Verbinde die beiden Satzteile mit "while" (zwei gleich lange Handlungen)!*

> Tom / watch TV - Dad / read his newspaper
> While Tom **was watching** TV, Dad **was reading** his newspaper.

a) Joe / learn English - Pat / play football
b) Ann / write a letter - Nelly / read a book
c) Sue / sleep - Tom / study English
d) Jim / pack his suitcase - Joe / work in the garden

3. *Bilde Sätze zu folgenden Bildern!*

> When the teacher **came** into the classroom
> Joe **was** sitting unter the Table.

a) Pat   b) Ann   c) Nelly   d) Jack and Sue

4. *Ergänze "NICHT WAHR?"*

a) Peter was singing a song, ... ?
b) Joe and Jack were dancing, ... ?
c) You were playing ball, ... ?
d) Ann was writing a test, ... ?
e) Sue and Nelly were sleeping, ... ?
f) Jane wasn't speaking English, ... ?
g) The children weren't learning French, ... ?

A. *Streiche den Buchstaben vor dem Wort durch, das in die Lücke paßt!*

> It's just as . . . in Vienna as in London.
> a) colder   b) coldest   c) colder than   d̶) cold

1. The green skirt is as . . . as the red skirt.
   a) cheaper   b) cheaper than   c) cheapest   d) cheap

2. A handbag is heavy. A rucksack is even . . .
   a) heaviest   b) heavier   c) as heavy   d) heavy

3. The weather in Berlin is . . . than in Rome.
   a) worse   b) bad   c) worst   d) as worse

4. Ann's pullover was . . . than Betty's.
   a) expensive   b) more expensive   c) as expensive   d) most expensive

5. What's the . . . thing to do when it is hot?
   a) good   b) best   c) better than   d) as good as

6. Tommy drank just a little milk. Jimmy drank even . . .
   a) less   b) little   c) least   d) less than

7. Betty is a beautiful girl. Mary is . . . than Betty.
   a) as beautiful   b) more beautiful   c) most beautiful   d) beautiful

8. The weather is fine today. It couldn't be . . .
   a) good   b) best   c) better   d) as good as

points: 8

B. *Ergänze jeweils die Zukunft!*

> Every summer Tom goes swimming. Next summer he *will go* swimming.

1. Jim writes a letter. Tomorrow he . . . two letters.
2. We learn English songs. Next week we . . . two English songs.
3. The children clean their teeth every morning. Tomorrow they . . . their teeth, too.
4. On Friday Mrs Brown bakes a cake. Tomorrow is Friday. She . . . a cake.
5. On Sunday Mr White washes his car. Tomorrow is Sunday. He . . . his car.
6. Every summer I read five books. Next summer I . . . some more.
7. Today the weather is fine. It . . . fine tomorrow, too.
8. Every winter the Millers travel to Austria. Next winter they . . . to Switzerland.

points: 8

C. *Welcher Satzteil stellt die kürzere, welcher die längere Handlung dar?*

> Mum *was reading* a book when Dad *came* home.
> (to read)   (to come)

1. Tom and Joe . . . football when the teacher . . . the classroom.
    (to play)   (to enter)
2. The telephone . . . when Joe . . . on the piano.
    (to ring)   (to play)   points: 4

D. Ersetze das unterstrichene Wort durch das "Stützwort"!

> Look at this pullover! Yes, the red *one* is very nice.

1. Joe wants black shoes and Sue wants white . . .
2. The red skirt is cheap but the green . . . is too expensive.
3. The blue coats are fashionable but the red . . . are too elegant.
4. Mary wrote a long letter, Tom wrote a short . . .

                                       points: 4

E. Setze ein: SOME – ANY!

1. Have you got . . . sweets?
2. Did you buy . . . jam?
3. Yes, we bought . . . jam.
4. We'd like . . . sugar.
5. We don't like . . . sweets!   points: 5

F. Setze ein: WHO – WHICH!

1. A baker is a person . . . bakes bread.
2. I don't like films . . . are boring.
3. Jane prefers puzzles . . . are difficult.
4. Here is the boy . . . wants to help you.
5. We'll take the train . . . arrives in Reading at 9.30.   points: 5

G. Das folgende Gespräch soll nicht wörtlich, sondern nur sinngemäß wiedergegeben werden! (2 Punkte pro Satz)

Die Verkäuferin fragt die Kundin, was sie für sie tun kann.	*What can I do for you?*
1. Mrs White sagt, sie hätte gern einen Rock.	
2. Die Verkäuferin bietet einen sehr schönen roten Rock an.	
3. Mrs White meint, er sei sehr schön, aber die Größe paßt nicht.	
4. Die Verkäuferin meint, das macht nichts, sie könnten ihn weiter machen.	

                                    points: 8

                                  A. - G.:   42

	very good	more revision needed
AHS, LG1	38 points and more	not even 32 points
LG 2	34 points and more	not even 28 points
LG 3	30 points and more	not even 24 points

Teacher: Whose satchel is this?
Tom: Which satchel?
Teacher: The one on the table!
Tom: It's [Peter's] .
         It's [his] .
Class: Yes, it belongs [to him] .

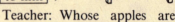

Teacher: Whose apples are these?
Ann: Which apples?
Teacher: The ones on the table!
Ann: They're [Betty's] .
         They're [hers] .
Class: Yes, they belong [to her] .

Teacher: Whose copy-books are these?
Tom and Ann: They're [ours] , madam!
               They belong [to us] .
Teacher: Whose book is this?
Jim: Oh, madam, . . . it's . . . it's [yours] ,
               madam! It belongs [to you] !
Teacher: Oh yes, it's [mine] . It belongs [to me] .

Beachte [die Angabe des Besitzes] !

. . . my **book**	mine	. . . our **car**	ours
. . . your **pen**	yours	. . . your **bike**	yours
. . . his **hat**	his	. . . their **house**	theirs
. . . her **ball**	hers		

| ↓ | ↓ | ↓ | ↓ |
| gefolgt vom **Hauptwort** | ohne Haupt-wort | gefolgt vom **Hauptwort** | ohne Haupt-wort |

1. Bilde Minidialoge nach folgendem Muster!

> A: Whose chair is this? Peter's?
> B: Yes, it's his chair. It's his.

a) pencil / Betty's
b) pencil-case / Sue's
c) copy-books / Ann's, John's

d) box / my box, Peter's
e) book / John's
f) ball / my ball, Jane's

2. Bilde Minidialoge nach folgendem Muster!

> A: Are these books yours or mine?
> B: I think, they're yours. Mine are over there.

a) pencils / his, hers
b) rubbers / ours, theirs

c) copy-books / mine, yours
d) pictures / yours, his

3. Bilde Dialoge nach folgendem Muster!
Beachte „Einzahl" – „Mehrzahl"

> A: Whose | book | is this?
> B: Which | book | ?
> A: The | one | in your satchel!
> B: It's <u>Jane's</u>. It belongs <u>to her</u>.

a) pencil-sharpener / in your pencil-case / Peter's
b) shoes / under the table / Mary's
c) box / on the table / Jim's and Betty's

4. Bilde möglichst viele sinnvolle Dialoge!

A: What are you doing with those two | balls?
pullovers?
fountain-pens?

B: One is mine and the other is | yours.
Peter's.
Betty's.

A: | me | hers.
Then give | him | mine.
| her | his.

93

36

DIFFERENT SCHOOLS –
THE SAME LESSONS

Franz attends the second form of a "Neue Hauptschule".
His friend Karl attends the second form of an "Allgemeinbildende höhere Schule".

Franz: We have four English lessons a week.
How often do you have English a week?
Karl: We have four English lessons, too.
How often do you have music?
Franz: We have two music lessons a week.
Karl: Let me have a look at your time-table!

	1st lesson	2nd lesson	3rd lesson	4th lesson	5th lesson	6th lesson	7th lesson	8th lesson
Monday	R.I.	History	English	German	Biology	P. E.		
Tuesday	English	Maths	History	German	Handicr.	Handicr.		
Wednesday	German	English	Art	Art	Geogr.		P. E.	P. E.
Thursday	Maths	English	German	Music	Physics	P. E.		Orchestra
Friday	German	Maths	English	Physics	Geogr.	R. I.		
Saturday	Maths	Music	Biology	History				

P. E. Physical Education   R. I. Religious Instruction   Geogr. Geography   Handicr. Handicraft

Franz: We have two music lessons a week, three history
lessons, two biology lessons, . . .
Karl: We have the same lessons, we've got the same
books, but we attend different schools! Why?

*1. Vergleiche deinen Stundenplan mit jenem von Franz und
schreibe deinen eigenen Stundenplan auf Englisch!*

2. Bilde Sätze nach folgendem Muster!

A: When do you have music?
B: I have music on Thursday in the fourth lesson and on
Saturday in the second lesson.

Verwende: biology, art, geography, religious instruction

3. Versuche Dialoge nach folgendem Muster!

> A: How often do you have English a week?
> B: Four times a week. We have four English lessons.

a) orchestra / once / one orchestra lesson
b) biology / twice / two biology lessons
c) history / three times / three history lessons
d) maths / four times / four maths lessons
e) German / five times / five German lessons

4. Sprich mit deinem Partner über einzelne Gegenstände!

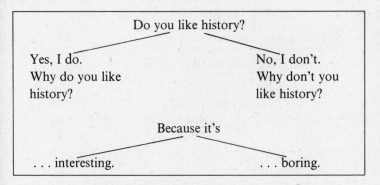

Do you like history?

Yes, I do.
Why do you like
history?

No, I don't.
Why don't you
like history?

Because it's

... interesting.   ... boring.

Verwende: too difficult, useful, (very) interesting, important, great fun, easy, useless, . . .

5. Löse das Rätsel! Das Wort im Kästchen hilft dir, untenstehenden Satz zu ergänzen!

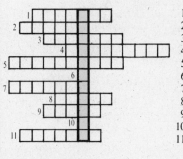

1. A language you learn
2. The language you speak
3. You learn about the Romans, . . .
4. You learn about countries, . . .
5. You work with a hammer, a saw, . . .
6. The fifth letter in the alphabet
7. You learn many important things
8. You work with numbers
9. You sing songs and play on instruments
10. The fourteenth letter in the alphabet
11. You learn about animals, . . .

School is always. . . . .

37

A LETTER FROM ENGLAND

Joe POTTER
42, Shelton Street

LONDON

January 10th, 19..

Dear Franz,

Thank you very much for your lovely

letter. I hope you are well.

You asked me about schools in England:

English schools start at nine.
English children wear a school uniform:
a blazer, a white blouse or a white shirt, and
a tie.
English children have their lunch at school.
They must stay until four.
There is no school on Saturdays.

I like German but I like maths better than German.

I like music best, it`s my favourite subject.

I must close now as I must do my homework.

Write soon.

Lots of love

Give my love to your parents!

Beachte!

I like ...   — I like ... better — I like ... best
ich mag ... — ich habe lieber — ich habe am liebsten

1. *Lies Joe's Brief sorgfältig durch! Vergleiche den Inhalt des Briefes mit folgenden Sätzen!*

	yes	no
Franz asked Joe about schools in England.	⊠	☐

a) English schools start at 10.
b) English children wear jeans at school.
c) English children stay until 4.
d) Joe goes to school on Saturdays.
e) Joe likes German.
f) Joe likes English best.

2. Bilde Sätze nach folgendem Muster!

> I like English. I like German **better** than English.
> I like art **best.** It's my favourite subject.

a) history — biology — geography
b) handicraft — physical education — physics
c) religious instruction — English — maths
d) art — music — history

3. Bilde Sätze nach folgendem Muster!

> Tom likes biology because it is interesting.
> He hates history because it is boring.

a) Ann: English / useful — physics / difficult
b) Sue and Ellen: art / great fun — maths / useless
c) Pat: geography / interesting — history / not important
d) What about you?

4. Schreibe einen Antwortbrief an Joe über deine Schule!

5. Versuche folgendes Gespräch auf Englisch!

Tom: fragt Sue nach ihrem Lieblingsgegenstand
Sue: sagt, sie hätte Englisch am liebsten
Tom: fragt nach dem Grund
Sue: sagt, Englisch sei interessant, nützlich und nicht schwierig

38

HAVE YOU DONE
YOUR EXERCISES YET?

Mum: Jim, where are you? Are you writing your exercises?

Jim: I've just written my exercises, Mum!

Betty: Really, Mum! Jim has already written his exercises!

Mum: Are you learning your poem by heart, Betty?

Betty: I've just learned my poem, Mum!

Jim: Really, Mum! Betty has already learned her poem!

Mum: Okay! Let me see your exercises, Jim!
Let me hear your poem, Betty!

Beachte die Vergangenheit (Present Perfect Tense) !

Bildung der Vergangenheit:

HAVE oder HAS + 3. Form des Zeitworts
(= Mittelwort der Vergangenheit
z.B. do — did — **done**
eat — ate — **eaten**)

I, you / we, you they HAVE	drunk done learned
He, she HAS	written eaten

↓
Mittelwort der
Vergangenheit

1. Übe die drei Formen des Zeitworts so, daß du jederzeit die dritte Form parat hast!

2. Ergänze jeweils die fehlenden Formen!

I break	I broke	I have broken
you . . .	you brought	you . . .
he . . .	he came	he . . .
she does	she . . .	she . . .
we . . .	we drank	we . . .
you . . .	you ate	you . . .
they find	they . . .	they . . .
I . . .	I got	I . . .
you give	you . . .	you . . .
he makes	he . . .	he . . .
she . . .	she read	she . . .

3. Bilde Minidialoge nach folgendem Muster!

A: **Have** you **done** your homework yet?
B: Yes, of course! I've already **done** it.

a) . . . eaten your bread . . .
b) . . . drunk your tea . . .
c) . . . cleaned your room . . .

4. Bilde Minidialoge nach folgendem Muster!

A: Are you reading your book?
B: I've already **read** my book.

a) Are you doing your homework?
b) Are you writing a letter to Granny?
c) Are you learning your new words?

5. Bilde Minidialoge nach folgendem Muster!

A: When will Peter read his book?
B: He **has** just **read** his book.

a) When will Peter do his homework?
b) When will Peter write a letter to Granny?
c) When will Peter learn his new words?

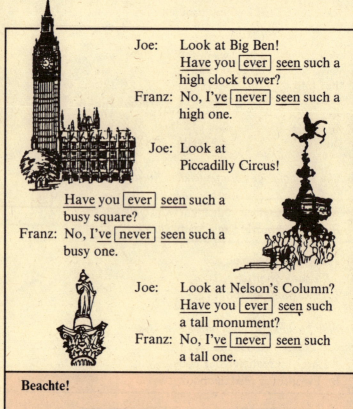

Joe: Look at Big Ben!
Have you ever seen such a high clock tower?

Franz: No, I've never seen such a high one.

Joe: Look at Piccadilly Circus!

Have you ever seen such a busy square?

Franz: No, I've never seen such a busy one.

Joe: Look at Nelson's Column?
Have you ever seen such a tall monument?

Franz: No, I've never seen such a tall one.

Beachte!

Have you	ever	seen. . .?	Hast du	jemals	. . .?
I have	never	seen. . .	Ich habe	niemals	. . .
He has	just	written. . .	Er hat	gerade.	. . .
She has	already	done. . .	Sie hat	schon	. . .

↓

„Signalwörter" verlangen die Vergangenheit

1. Bilde Sätze nach folgendem Muster!

Tom is taking a photo.
Have you ever taken a photo?

a) Jim is speaking English.
b) Pat is asking a policeman.
c) Joe is driving a car.
d) Sue is running to the station.
e) Sandy is drinking whisky.

2. *Lies das Gespräch im Kästchen gut durch!*
   Versuche ähnliche Dialoge zu folgenden Bildern!

a)
The National
Gallery/
an interesting
museum

b)
The Tower /
an old castle

c)
St. Martin's-in-
the-Fields /
an interesting
church

3. *Bilde Dialoge nach folgendem Muster!*

> ① ②
> A: We've just **bought a book.** It's very **interesting.**
> ③
> B: I've never **read** such an interesting book.
>   It's the most interesting one I've ever read.

	①	②	③
a)	seen a film	exciting	seen
b)	eaten an ice-cream	fine	eaten
c)	crossed Oxford Street	busy	seen
d)	watched "Changing the Guard"	funny	watched (spectacle)

4. *Versuche folgendes Gespräch auf Englisch!*

A: fragt Joe, ob er jemals eine so interessante Brücke gesehen
   habe
B: verneint, er habe noch nie eine so interessante Brücke
   gesehen: sie sei wirklich die interessanteste Brücke, die er je
   gesehen habe

Invitation to Johnny's special party Febr. 15

Every guest must bring something he doesn't want or need, every guest must buy something.

On February 15th Johnny's house was full of people:

"Look at this old doll!
I've never seen a nicer one!"
"Yes, it's really the nicest doll
I've ever seen!"

"Have you already seen such a lovely toy train?"
"I've just seen this lovely toy train. It's really lovely!"

1. Lies den Text im Kästchen gut durch!
Vergleiche mit folgenden Sätzen!

	yes	no
It was a special party.	☒	☐

a) It took place on January 15th.
b) It was Peter's party.
c) Every guest must bring something he likes very much.
d) Every guest must buy something.
e) There were not many people.
f) There was a nice old doll.
g) There was a lovely toy train.

2. Bilde Sätze nach folgendem Muster!

> Mary didn't want her old doll, so she brought her doll.

a) Nelly: ball
b) Joe: toy train

c) Frank: toy car
d) Sue and Ann: camera

3. Bilde Dialoge nach folgendem Muster!

> A: Just have a look at this nice camera!
> B: I've never seen a nicer one!
> A: Yes, it's really the nicest camera I've ever seen.

a) funny kite
b) nice lamp

c) nice toy car
d) beautiful chess set

4. Beachte "bought" – "brought"! Ergänze jeweils die Kurzantwort!

a) Has Peter bought anything? No, . . .
b) Have you brought anything? Yes, . . .
c) Has Mary brought anything? Yes, . . .
d) Has Tom bought anything? No, . . .
e) Has Mary bought the toy train? No, . . .

5. Ergänze jeweils "NICHT WAHR?"!

a) Peter hasn't bought anything, . . . ?
b) You have brought the toy train, . . . ?
c) Mary has brought the doll, . . . ?
d) Tom and Joe haven't bought anything, . . . ?
e) Jim has bought a ball, . . . ?

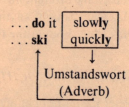

Sue: Look here, Fred!
 I've just learned to do
 the snow-plough.
Fred: You a r e a slow skier, Sue!
Sue: I'll do it <u>slowly</u> at the beginning.
Fred: Look at me! I'm a good skier. I'm in the first
 group. I can ski <u>well</u>.

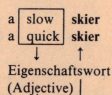

Sue: Can you show me how to
 stop, Fred?
Fred: Oh, I can stop <u>quickly</u> -
 I just kiss the snow!

Beachte!

a | slow | skier
a | quick | skier
↓
Eigenschaftswort
(Adjective)

...**do** it | slowly
...**ski** | quickly
↓
Umstandswort
(Adverb)

nähere Bestimmung
des **Hauptwortes**
"Wie ist es?"

nähere Bestimmung
des **Zeitwortes**
"Wie **wird** es **gemacht?**"

Bildung des Umstandswortes:
- Regelmäßig durch Anhängen der Nachsilbe "-ly":
 slow - slow**ly**, quick - quick**ly**
- Merke! friendly - **in a friendly way**
 fast - **fast**
 good - **well**

104

- Umstandswörter mit 2 Formen unterschiedlicher Bedeutung:

hard (schwer)	-	hardly (kaum)
near (nahe)	-	nearly (fast, beinahe)
late (spät)	-	lately (neulich, unlängst)

1. *Lies das Gespräch im Kästchen gut durch!*
   Beachte „slowly, well, quickly" und unterstreiche das zugehörige Zeitwort!

2. *Eigenschaftswort oder Umstandswort? Ergänze die Lücken!*

a) quick - quickly: Tom runs . . . He is a . . . runner.
b) polite - politely: Peter is a . . . boy. He greets . . .
c) bad - badly: Ann skis . . . She is a . . . skier.
d) beautiful - beautifully: Jane is a . . . girl. But she doesn't sing . . .
e) easy - easily: Skiing is . . . Tom learned it . . .
f) fast - fast: Fred is a . . . skier. Yes, he skis . . .
g) good - well: Sue is a . . . girl. She can't ski . . .

3. *Setze ein: hard – hardly!*

a) Joe . . . goes to football matches.
b) Dad works . . .
c) His friend . . . works.
d) Are the children working . . . ?

4. *Setze ein: near – nearly!*

a) Pat . . . missed the bus.
b) Ann lives . . . the theatre.
c) Uncle Fred . . . visited us.
d) Dad . . . bought that expensive car.

5. *Setze ein: late – lately!*

a) Are you . . . for school?
b) I haven't been to the theatre . . .
c) Joe arrived . . . last Sunday.
d) We haven't talked to him . . .

Reporter:
Let's have a look at the girls!

Ann is skiing carefully, not quickly!
Alice is skiing more carefully!
And what about Ellen? — Where is she?
Oh, she's skiing most carefully of all!
What a pity! All the girls are skiing
too slowly to win a prize!

And what about the boys?
Jim is skiing fast.
Joe is skiing faster.
John is skiing fastest of all!
He is the winner!

SCHOOL COMPETITION

Beachte die Steigerung des Umstandswortes!

- Einsilbige Umstandswörter steigern auf -er, -est:

  fast - faster - fastest
  hard - harder - hardest

- Mehrsilbige Umstandswörter steigern mit "more" und "most":

  beautifully - more beautifully - most beautifully

- Unregelmäßige Steigerung:

  well - better - best
  badly - worse - worst

1. Gib die Steigerung folgender Umstandswörter an!

beautifully - . . . - . . .   quickly - . . . - . . .
fast - . . . - . . .   badly - . . . - . . .
well - . . . - . . .   slowly - . . . - . . .

2. Lies die Reportage im Kästchen gut durch!
   Übernimm selbst die Rolle des Reporters und ersetze

a) carefully durch "slowly"
b) fast durch "quickly"!

3. Bilde Sätze nach folgendem Muster!

> Who skied fastest?
> Ann skied fast.
> Jim skied faster.
> Tom skied fastest.

b)

Jim   Joe   Ann

a) Who ran most slowly?
b) Who skated best?
c) Who played worst?

a)    c)

Sue   Betty   Sandy   Jim   Joe   John

4. Bilde Sätze nach folgendem Muster!

> Who skied fastest?
> It was Tom who skied fastest.

Verwende die Angaben von Nr. 3 a) b) c).

5. Bilde Dialoge nach folgendem Muster!

> Why did Joe win the first prize?
> Because he skied fastest.

a) Pat / win the competition / ran most quickly
b) Ann / get a good mark / wrote . . . most carefully
c) Sue / get a bad mark / painted . . . worst
d) Joe / arrive in time / got up earliest
e) Jim / kiss the snow / skied most carelessly

43

A NEW PUPIL

Teacher: Good morning, girls and boys!
Children: Good morning, madam!

Teacher: This is Anica, a new pupil in our class.

Tom: Where are you from, Anica?

Anica: I'm from Yugoslavia. I lived in Belgrade.

Mary: And what is your full name?

Anica: Anica Kostič.

Jane: Have you got any brothers or sisters?

Anica: Oh yes, I've got two brothers but no sister.

Jim: Have you ever been to Vienna before?

Anica: No, never! But three years ago I stayed in
           Graz. Last summer I was in Salzburg.

Teacher: So you know a lot about Austria. And -
           by the way - you speak English quite well.

Anica: But I'm afraid, my German won't be good
           enough to understand my German teacher!

Beachte!

Signalwörter

AGO, LAST → Past Tense

EVER, NEVER → Present Perfect Tense

---

1. Lies das Gespräch im Kästchen gut durch, dann kreuze die richtige Antwort an!

This is Anica, a new . . . in our class.
a) pupil   b) boy   c) girl

She is from . . .
a) Italy   b) England   c) Yugoslavia

Anica lived in . . .
a) Graz   b) Belgrade   c) Vienna

She has got two . . .
a) friends   b) sisters   c) brothers

She stayed in Graz three . . . ago.
a) weeks   b) months   c) years

She speaks . . . quite well.
a) English   b) German   c) French

2. Versuche Dialoge nach folgendem Muster!

> A: Have you ever been to Belgrade before?
> B: No, never. But two years ago I stayed in Krk.

a) Reading / four months ago / in Oxford
b) Innsbruck / two years ago / in Schwaz
c) Paris / five years ago / in Nice
d) Munich / six weeks ago / in Rosenheim

3. Bilde Dialoge nach folgendem Muster!

> A: You speak German quite well!
> B: But I'm afraid my German won't be good enough
>   to understand the people in Vienna.

a) English / London   c) Greek / Athens
b) Italian / Rome   d) Spanish / Madrid

*4. Schreibe einen Bericht über die neue Schülerin in deiner
Klasse! Folgende Fragen helfen dir dabei!*

a) Where did she come from?
b) What is her name?
c) What do you know about her family?
d) Does she speak English well?

Beginne: There's a new pupil in our class.

HOW TO MAKE A CAKE

Tom: Sandy's birthday is on the 20th of March.
Let's make a fine cake for her!

Joe: Let's have a look into mother's cookery-book!
It says:

Ingredients:
3 eggs
200 gr. butter
200 gr. sugar
200 gr. flour
some baking-powder

Put the butter and the sugar into a basin. Beat them with your electric beater. Put the eggs into the basin. Beat them. Then pour the flour and the baking-powder into the basin. Beat them. Fill the tin from the basin. Then put it into the oven (220° C.) Take the cake out after 35 minutes.

Tom: All right - we'll try this cake.

1. Lies das Rezept gut durch und unterstreiche alle Zeitwörter!

2. Ergänze bei den folgenden Zeitwörtern jeweils die zweite und dritte Form!

to put   - . . . - . . .
to beat   - . . . - . . .
to pour - . . . - . . .
to fill   - . . . - . . .
to take   - . . . - . . .

3. Joe erklärt Tom, wie der Kuchen zubereitet werden soll!

When you have put the butter and the sugar into a basin, you beat them with your electric beater.

Setze fort: When you have beaten . . .

4. *Bilde Dialoge nach folgendem Muster!*

> Tom: Have you already put the butter and the sugar into the basin?
> Joe: I've just put the butter and the sugar into the basin.

Setze fort: Have you already beaten . . .

5. *Bilde Dialoge nach folgendem Muster!*

> Tom: Have you put the butter and the sugar into the basin?
> Joe: No, I have forgotten to put the butter into the basin.

Setze fort: Have you beaten them . . .

6. *Sandys Geburtstagskuchen wird bestaunt!*

> A: Have you ever **seen** such a fine cake?
> B: No, I've never **seen** such a fine cake.

Verwende: eaten, prepared, tried, smelled, tasted, got, . . .

7. *Welche Sätze stimmen mit den Angaben im Kästchen zu Beginn des Kapitels überein?*

	yes	no
Sandy's birthday is on the 20th of April.	☐	☒

a) Ingredients: 5 eggs, . . . ☐ ☐
b) Put the flour and the eggs into a basin. ☐ ☐
c) Take the cake out after 35 minutes. ☐ ☐
d) Ingredients: no baking-powder ☐ ☐
e) Tom and Joe won't try this cake. ☐ ☐

IT'S THE BEST FILM
THAT I'VE EVER SEEN!

Joe: Can you come to "Covent Garden" with me tonight? "Romeo and Juliet" is the best ballet that I've ever seen!

COLISEUM
SADLER'S WELLS OPERA
Evening's 7.30
Box Office TEM 3161.
Tues. & Fri.
LA TRAVIATA
Wed. & Sat. (major revival)
MADAM BUTTERFLY
Thurs.
THE FLYING DUTCHMAN
Covent Garden, The Royal Ballet
Wed. & Fri. at 7.30
ROMEO AND JULIET
Thurs. at 7.30 SWAN LAKE

9.00 NEWS, WEATHER.
9.25 THE SECRET SERVANT
11.25 — 11.55 BUONGIORNO
ITALIA!
Italian for beginners
12.00 Paul McCARTNEY:
The Man, His Music,
His Movies.

Betty: That's really a good idea! But I wanted to watch "Buongiorno Italia". It's the best course for beginners that I've ever heard.

Everything that is on TV 1 is interesting!

Beachte das bezügliche Fürwort !

THAT < steht anstelle von WHO oder WHICH!
muß stehen nach:

— the best, the tallest, the most beautiful, . . .
(letzte Steigerungsstufe)
— Wörtern wie: all, everything, something, nothing . . .
— "Mr Brown and his dog . . . ", "Susan and her doll . . ." (Personen und Tiere/Dinge gemeinsam)

1. *Lies den Dialog im Kästchen gut durch!*
   Versuche ähnliche Gespräche!

a) . . . to the "Coliseum" . . . / La Traviata / opera /
   . . . "The Secret Servant" / the best film

b) . . . to "Covent Garden" . . . / Swan Lake / ballet /
   . . . "Paul McCartney" / the best documentary

2. *Bilde Dialoge nach folgendem Muster!*

A: Is this film interesting? Have you seen it?
B: Yes, it's the **most interesting** film **that** I've ever seen.

---

a) play / amusing / seen
b) book / boring / read
.c) story / funny / heard
d) puzzle / difficult / tried

3. *Setze ein, WHO, WHICH, THAT!*

a) Mr Miller bought everything . . . was on sale.
b) Here is the boy . . . won the first prize.
c) They were looking for the book . . . was on the shelf.
d) This is the most interesting story . . . I have ever read.
e) This is the present . . . I bought for Nelly.
f) Yes, it's the most expensive present . . . I've ever bought.
g) Is there anything . . . we can do for you?
h) This is the girl . . . sang the beautiful songs.
i) This is the most beautiful girl . . . I have ever seen.
j) All . . . he said was true.

4. *Ein Ratespiel!*

I'm thinking of **something that** is green.
Is it a thing / a person / a flower, . . . ?
Yes, it is. - No, it isn't.

Sieger ist derjenige, der die wenigsten Fragen stellen muß!

A. Ergänze die Sätze nach folgendem Muster!

> Are you doing your exercises?   I *have done* them!

1. Is Tom writing a letter? He . . . it!
2. Are you baking a cake? I . . . a cake!
3. Are the children learning English? They . . . English!
4. Are Tom and Ann drinking their tea? They . . . it!
5. Are you reading a book? I . . . it!
6. Is Mary watching TV? She . . . TV!
7. Is Joe eating his soup? He . . . it!
8. Are the Millers washing their car? They . . . it!   points: 8

B. Ergänze die Sätze nach folgendem Muster!

> Is this hat Tom's?   Yes, it's *his*.

1. Is this book Mary's? Yes, it's . . .
2. Are these balls the children's. No, they aren't . . .
3. Does this cap belong to you? Yes, it's . . .
4. These books belong to us. They are . . .
5. This house belongs to me. It's . . .
6. Here is Peter's copy-book. It's . . .   points: 6

C. Eigenschaftswort oder Umstandswort? Ergänze die Lücken!

> quick: Peter is a *quick* boy. He skis *quickly*.

1. easy: Skiing is . . . Jane learned it . . .
2. fast: Father is a . . . driver. He drives . . .
3. good: Tom wrote this test . . . He got a . . . mark.
4. bad: Sue is a . . . skier. Yes, she skis . . .
5. slow: He does his work . . . He is a . . . worker.
6. friendly: Tom greets us . . . He is a . . . boy.   points: 6

D. Beachte die Bedeutung der Umstandswörter! Ergänze die Lücken!

late - lately:
1. Joe arrived . . . last night.
2. We haven't been to the cinema . . .

hard - hardly:
3. Joe . . . goes to the cinema.
4. The children worked . . . in class.

near - nearly:
5. We . . . missed the bus.
6. Tom lives . . . the station.   points: 6

E. Ergänze die Lücken: WHO – WHICH – THAT

1. This is the boy . . . won the first prize.
2. All . . . she said was untrue.
3. This is the tallest building . . . I've ever seen.
4. Is there anything . . . we can do for you?
5. This is the book . . . I bought for Nelly.
6. This is the most expensive car . . . I've ever seen.
7. Here is the girl . . . can sing English songs.
8. I'm thinking of something . . . is red.

points: 8

F. Das folgende Gespräch soll nicht wörtlich, sondern nur sinngemäß wiedergegeben werden! (2 Punkte pro Satz)

Franz sagt, er habe 4 Englisch-stunden pro Woche.	*I have four English lessons a week.*
1. Karl fragt Franz, wie oft pro Woche er Geographie habe.	
2. Franz sagt, 2 x pro Woche habe er Geographie.	
3. Karl sagt, er würde gern den Stundenplan von Franz sehen.	
4. Franz und Karl stellen erstaunt fest, sie haben die gleichen Stunden.	

points: 8

A. - F: 42

	very good	more revision needed
AHS, LG1	38 points and more	not even 32 points
LG 2	34 points and more	not even 28 points
LG 3	30 points and more	not even 24 points

WHAT WOULD YOU DO IF . . . ?

Ann: What would you do <u>if you were</u> rich?

Jane: Well, <u>I'd make</u> a journey . . . to London perhaps.
And <u>what would you do</u> <u>if you had</u> a lot of money?

Ann: <u>If I had</u> a lot of money, <u>I'd buy</u> a big car.

Jane: First we should buy a car, then travel to London.

Beachte die **IF-SÄTZE (Bedingungssätze / Conditionals)!**

If he $\boxed{had}$ money, he $\boxed{would}$ buy a bike.

Wenn er . . . $\boxed{hätte}$, $\boxed{würde}$ er . . . kaufen.

If I $\boxed{were}$ rich, I $\boxed{should}$ travel to London.

Wenn ich . . . $\boxed{wäre}$, $\boxed{würde}$ ich . . . reisen.

Das gesprochene Englisch unterscheidet nicht zwischen
"would" und "should"!

I **should** buy	=	I'd buy	
You would buy	=	You'd buy	
He / she would buy	=	He / she'd buy	ich, du, er . . .
We **should** buy	=	We'd buy	**WÜRDE**
You would buy	=	You'd buy	kaufen
They would buy	=	They'd buy	

Achtung!

Im IF-SATZ steht in **allen Personen WERE** (wäre)
If I were . . . , If you were . . . , If he were . . .

1. Was würdest du tun, wenn . . . ?

If I had a lot of money, If I were rich,	I'd	buy a house. travel round the world. buy a horse. help the poor.

2. Bilde möglichst viele sinnvolle Sätze!

If Tom If Ann If we	were rich, had time,	he she we	'd	go to the cinema. play tennis. buy a house. go to the theatre.

3. Verbinde die beiden Sätze zu einem IF-SATZ!

> The weather is fine. We can go swimming.
> But it isn't fine!
> If the weather were fine, we could go swimming.

a) We have time. We can go to the cinema.
    But we have no time!
b) Tom is at school. He can meet his friends.
    But he isn't at school!
c) I am rich. I can buy a car.
    But I am not rich!
d) Betty is in the garden. She can play ball.
    But she isn't in the garden!

4. Bilde Dialoge nach folgendem Muster!

> A: Can she pass the test? Is she really so clever?
> B: If she were clever, she'd pass the test.

a) Can he win the prize? Is he really so fast?
b) Can she ski down that slope? Is she really so courageous?
c) Can he play the piano? Is he really so musical?
d) Can she carry that sack? Is she really so strong?

117

P	D
X	

Don't walk on the road!

You must not play in the street!

Don't use your skateboard on the road!

Don't cycle on the wrong side of the road!

You must not forget to keep to the left in England!

Don't go when the sign says "STOP"!

Don't forget to look right and left!

Don't read the newspaper when you cross the road!

You must not overtake cars on a narrow road.

Don't cross the road when the sign is RED or AMBER!

red: „stop"
amber: „caution"
green: „go"

Beachte das Verbot!
DON'T (= DO NOT) . . . "tu es nicht!"
YOU MUST NOT . . . . "du darfst nicht"

1. Lies die Verkehrsregeln gut durch! Welche gelten für Fußgeher, welche für Autofahrer, welche für beide?

Kreuze an: P = Pedestrians (Fußgeher)
  D = Driver (Autofahrer)

2. Bilde Dialoge nach folgendem Muster!

> A: Mum, I want to go out!
> B: All right! But don't walk on the road!
>   You must not walk on the road!

Verwende: play in the street, use your skateboard on the road, cycle on the wrong side of the road, go when the sign says "STOP"

3. Was ist hier verboten?

> What does this traffic sign tell us?
> It says, "You must not turn left!"

a)
turn

b)
overtake

c)
stop

d)
drive fast

4. Bilde Sätze nach folgendem Muster!

> The policeman says, "You may play in the park, but you must not play on the road."

a) . . . use your skateboard in the park, but . . .
b) . . . cross the road when the traffic light is green . . .
c) . . . cycle on the left side . . .
d) . . . go when the traffic light says "GO" . . .
e) . . . walk on the pavement . . .

5. Setze ein: quick – quickly, slow – slowly, careful – carefully

a) You are a . . . boy. Cross the road . . . !
b) You must drive . . . here! Don't forget to be . . . !
c) Look . . . ! You must be . . . when you cross the road.
d) Look right and left, then run . . . ! Be . . . !
e) Drive . . . at the beginning! You must be . . . here!

Tom: Just look at the plan of our new house!

Joe: Your new house is quite comfortable, isn't it?

Tom: Yes, but there's quite a lot of work to do!
We <u>must</u> clean all the windows.
We <u>must</u> hang up all the curtains, . . .
Yesterday I <u>had to</u> clean all the doors and I <u>had to</u> vacuum the staircase.

Joe: Your living room is very nice, too!

Tom: Yes, of course, it is! I'm glad we haven't got the carpets yet, so <u>we need not</u> vacuum the carpets.

·**Beachte!**

Da man vom Wort MUST (= müssen) **nicht** alle Zeiten bilden kann, gibt es eine **Ersatzform** (= **TO HAVE TO . . .**)

Gegenwart: Ersatzform		**Mitvergangenheit:** nur Ersatzform!
I must	= I have to . . .	I had to . . .
You must	= You have to . . .	You had to . . .
He must	= He **has** to . . .	He had to . . .
She must	= She **has** to . . .	She had to . . .
We must	= We have to . . .	We had to . . .
You must	= You have to . . .	You had to . . .
They must	= They have to . .	They had to . . .

Unterscheide!
You MUST . . . . du mußt
You MUST NOT . . . du **darfst nicht** (Verbot!)
You NEED NOT . . . du mußt nicht, du brauchst nicht,
(es ist nicht notwendig)

1. Bilde Sätze nach folgendem Muster!

> A: Must we clean the windows now?
> B: Yes, you have to clean them now.

Verwende: vacuum the floor, wash the glasses, paint the windows, dust the chairs, polish the floor, . . .

2. Bilde Sätze nach folgendem Muster!

> A: Must we clean the windows now?
> B: Oh no, you don't have to clean them now.

Verwende die Angaben von Nr. 1!

3. Das neue Haus macht viel Arbeit!

> Yesterday I had to paint the doors.
> Today I have to paint the windows.

a) . . . to paper the living room / bed room
b) . . . to clean the windows / doors
c) . . . to vacuum the floor / armchairs
d) . . . to wash the glasses / the pots and pans
e) . . . to install the fuse boxes / water-taps

4. Bilde Sätze nach folgendem Muster!

> Today Joe has to paint the doors
> Yesterday he had to paint the windows.

Verwende die Angaben von Nr. 3!

5. Bilde Sätze nach folgendem Muster!

> You must tidy the room, but you need not make the beds.

a) wash the cups / the glasses
b) polish the floor / the furniture
c) vacuum the staircase / the armchairs
d) dust the furniture / the windows

49

LET'S HELP THE FARMER!

Uncle Fred: Look, Tom and Mary! This is our new cowshed ... and here is our new sty. Tom, you're a big boy, you <u>can</u> help me! You <u>can</u> feed the pigs. You <u>can</u> milk the cows, ... Mary, you're a big girl, you <u>can</u> help me, too! You <u>can</u> water the flowers. You <u>can</u> clean the sty, ...

Tom: Oh, Uncle Fred! I could feed the pigs.

| But I | could not | milk the cows, |
| I really | wasn't able to | milk the cows! |

Mary: I could water the flowers.

| But I | could not | clean the sty, |
| I really | wasn't able to | clean the sty! |

Tom and Mary: Uncle Fred, we are so sorry,

| we | could not | help you. |
| We | were not able to | help you! |

Beachte!
Vom Wort CAN können **nicht** alle Zeiten gebildet werden. **Ersatzform: TO BE ABLE TO . . .**

Gegenwart:		Ersatzform
I can	=	I am able to . . .
You can	=	You are able to . . .
He / she can	=	He / she is able to . . .
We / you / they can	=	We / you / they are able to . . .

Mitvergangenheit:		Ersatzform:
I could	=	I was able to . . .
You could	=	You were able to . . .
He / she could	=	He / she was able to . . .
We / you / they could	=	We / you / they were able to

In der Gegenwart und Mitvergangenheit besteht **zwischen CAN und Ersatzform**, bzw. **COULD und Ersatzform** ein **Bedeutungsunterschied!**

CAN . . . . können
TO BE ABLE TO . . . fähig sein, imstande sein

1. *Lies das Gespräch im Kästchen gut durch! Beachte den Bedeutungsunterschied zwischen CAN und TO BE ABLE TO ...!*

2. *Bilde Dialoge nach folgendem Muster!*

> A: Jim, you can cut the grass!
> B: I'm sorry, I can't cut the grass, I'm really not able to cut the grass.

Verwende: feed the hens, bring in the hay, repair the tractor, clean the harvester, clean the cowshed, ...

3. *Bilde Sätze nach folgendem Muster! Angaben von Nr. 2!*

> Last summer little Tom couldn't help the farmer.
> This summer he can help him.

4. *Bilde Sätze nach folgendem Muster! Angaben von Nr. 2!*

> Nelly was able to cut the grass.
> Can you cut the grass?

5. *Beachte: Gegenwart – Mitvergangenheit!*
   Ergänze die Lücken!

a) Last summer Uncle Fred _____ bring in the hay.
   (konnte nicht)

b) Little Tom _____ reach the apples,
   (ist nicht imstande)
   he isn't tall enough.

c) Aunt Betty _____ clean the sty today.
   (kann nicht)

d) Yesterday she _____ clean the sty.
   (war nicht imstande)

e) All the children _____ help the farmer.
   (können)

f) Uncle Fred _____ repair the tractor.
   (war nicht imstande)

50

JOE'S BIRTHDAY - A DAY OF BAD LUCK!

Joe's greatest wish was to get roller-skates for his 12th birthday.

So Dad bought roller-skates and a safety equipment: a helmet and knee pads for Joe.

When Joe got his birthday presents he was so happy that he tried the roller-skates out at once.
But he forgot something very important:
he didn't put on his helmet and he didn't take his knee pads.

Joe went to the park - the new roller-skates were fantastic!

Suddenly two big dogs came out from behind the trees. Joe <u>couldn't stop</u> - he fell!

He hurt his knees and elbows so that he <u>wasn't able to get up.</u>
An ambulance took Joe to hospital.

Joe's 12th birthday - a day of bad luck!

Beachte den Bedeutungsunterschied zwischen CAN und der Ersatzform!

1. *Lies diese Geschichte gut durch! Welche der folgenden Sätze stimmen mit den Angaben im Kästchen überein.*

	yes	no
It was Joe's 13th birthday.	☐	☒

a) Dad bought a skateboard.
b) Joe was very happy.
c) He put on his helmet.

	yes	no
a)	☐	☐
b)	☐	☐
c)	☐	☐

	yes	no
d) The roller-skates were too slow.	☐	☐
e) Joe could stop.	☐	☐
f) He wasn't able to get up.	☐	☐

2. Bilde Sätze nach folgendem Muster!

> A: Joe can stop.
> B: I bet Joe isn't able to stop.

a) Joe can get up.
b) Joe can play tennis.
c) Joe can go boating.
d) Joe can come with us.
e) Joe can help us.

3. Bilde Sätze nach folgendem Muster!

> A: Joe could not stop.
> B: Why was he not able to stop?

a) He could not get up.
b) He could not play football.
c) He could not go to school.
d) He could not practise roller-skating.
e) He could not come with us.

4. Setze ein: Must – must not!

a) You . . . forget your helmet.
b) You . . . take your knee pads.
c) You . . . be careful.
d) You . . . skate too fast.
e) You . . . skate on the road.

5. Joe berichtet in einem Brief über seinen Unfall

> Dear Jack,
>   My greatest wish was . . .

Jim: Hello, Peter, what did you do last Sunday?

Peter: We went on an outing! We walked through the woods and wanted to have a picnic, but the resting place was polluted. There were plastic bags, empty tins, empty bottles, but there was no refuse bin . . . so we walked on.

Jim: And what did you do then?

Peter: At last we arrived at a little lake and wanted to swim. But the water was too dirty — it was just the same all over again: waste and rubbish everywhere! So we came home earlier than usual.

Jim: And what can y o u do against pollution?

1. *Lies das Gespräch im Kästchen gut durch und überlege, was du gegen Umweltverschmutzung tun kannst!*

2. *Welche der folgenden Sätze geben den Sinn des Gesprächs im Kästchen wieder?*

	yes	no
Peter went to school.	☐	☒

a) He picked some flowers.
b) The resting place was polluted.
c) There were no plastic bags.
d) There was a refuse bin.
e) At last they arrived at a river.
f) The water was very fine.
g) They came home later than usual.

126

3. *Stelle diejenigen Sätze richtig, die du in Aufgabe 2 mit "No"
gekennzeichnet hast!*

> Peter didn't go to school. He went on an outing.

4. *Bilde Sätze nach folgendem Muster!*

> A: Let's throw away the empty bottles!
> B: No, you must not throw away the empty bottles!

Verwende: . . . the plastic bags,
 . . . the empty tins,
 . . . the paper bags, . . .

5. *Bilde Minidialoge nach folgendem Muster!*

> A: Did you throw away the empty bottles?
> B: No, I didn't.

Verwende die Angaben von Nr. 4!

6. *Bilde Dialoge nach folgendem Muster!*

> A: Why did you throw away the empty bottles?
> B: Sorry, I'll collect them and put them into the
> refuse bin.

Verwende die Angaben von Nr. 4!

At the end of the school year the children wanted to organize a party.

All the girls and boys talked at the same time:

— Let's invite all our friends!
— Perhaps we could invite all our teachers!
— I think we could organize a match!

— Yes, that's a good idea!
— No, that's nonsense!
— Oh, yes, let's do that!

— It would be fine to have some orange juice!
— We should prepare sandwiches!
— We could make a cake!

— I don't like that!
— That's stupid!
— Oh, fantastic!

Beachte!
"Vorschläge machen" auf Englisch!

Let's . . .
We could . . .
We should . . .
It would be fine / nice . . .

1. *Aus den Angaben im Kästchen kannst du 81 verschiedene Dialoge zusammenstellen! Jeder beliebige Satz aus dem ersten Block ist mit jedem beliebigen Satz des zweiten Blocks u.s.w. zu kombinieren.*

2. *Bilde Sätze nach folgendem Muster!*

> Last summer the children had a party.
> Next summer they will have a party, too.

Verwende: invite all their friends,
organize a match,
prepare sandwiches,
make a cake,
have orange juice, . . .

3. *Bilde möglichst viele Sätze!*

We could prepare Let's have	some	coffee. sandwiches. juice. cake.

4. *Die Kinder laden dich telefonisch zur Party ein!*

Tom: Hello, . . . , this is Tom speaking.
Can you come to our party?
. . . : Oh, yes, . . . When . . . ?
Tom: Next Monday, 6 o'clock.
. . . : Where . . . ?
Tom: At school, in our classroom.
. . . : That's really . . . I'd like . . .
Thank you! . . .
Tom: . . .

5. *Versuche folgende Sätze auf Englisch wiederzugeben!*

a) Vielleicht könnten wir einige belegte Brote vorbereiten.
b) Laden wir die Millers ein!
c) Wir sollten etwas Fruchtsaft vorbereiten!

Betty: We'll fly to London on the thirteenth of June. I think we should pack our suitcases!

Tom: Yes, that's right - but where is my suitcase? Is it on the cupboard? Is it under the bed?

Betty: Oh no, my suitcase is behind the boxes in the storage room, yours is beside mine.

Tom: Let's look for all the other things!

Betty: Don't forget the book we've bought for our English friends!

Tom: Yes, it's a book about Vienna.

Betty: Do you remember our last trip to London?

Tom: We haven't been there since 1982.

Betty: We haven't been in London for many years.

Tom: I'm looking forward   to our holidays. And what about you?

Beachte die Vorwörter (Präpositionen / Prepositions)!

am 30. Juni .... **on** the thirtieth **of** June.
suchen .... to look **for** ...
ein Buch über .... a book **about** ...
sich auf etwas freuen ... to look **forward to** ...

SEIT

since (gibt den Beginn einer Handlung an, ... seit 1982)

for (gibt den Zeitraum an, ... seit vielen Jahren)

1. *Setze ein:* on, in, under, behind, by, between, since, for, to about!

a) Nelly is sitting . . . Tom and Peter.
b) Where are my pencils? They are . . . your pencil-case.
c) I haven't spoken English . . . Monday.
d) We go . . . school . . . bus.
e) This book is very interesting. Yes, it's a book . . . London.
f) Jim is sitting in front of Joe. Joe is . . . Jim.
g) Can you come . . . Sunday?
h) We haven't spoken English . . . three days.

2. *Setze die fehlenden Vorwörter ein!*

a) Who is that man . . . you? (neben dir)
   That's Mr White. His wife is . . . me. (hinter mir)

b) The children aren't . . . school. (in der Schule)
   They are . . . home. (zu Hause)

c) I haven't watched TV . . . days. (seit Tagen)
   The programme . . . Sunday was not so bad. (am Sonntag)

d) I've bought a book . . . Austria. (über Österreich)
   But I can't find it. I must look . . . it. (es suchen)

e) I'm looking forward . . . my holidays. (auf meine Ferien)
   We'll travel . . . England. (nach England)

3. *Setze ein: „seit"!*

a) I haven't seen him . . . five days.
b) I haven't met the Millers . . . June 3rd.
c) We haven't been in London . . . 3 years.
d) The Coopers haven't been in London . . . 1980.
e) Jim has been in Italy . . . 1968.
f) Mary has been in Greece . . . two weeks.

Aunt Mary:	Would you like tea, coffee or cocoa?
Betty:	Just a little tea, please.
Tom:	I'd like coffee, please — but not too <u>much</u> coffee!
Aunt Mary:	Would you like a piece of bread?
Tom:	No, thank you, I'd like a roll.
Aunt Mary:	Oh, sorry, there are only <u>a few</u> rolls left. I didn't buy <u>many</u> rolls yesterday. What about some porridge?
Tom and Betty:	No, thank you!
Aunt Mary:	I can offer you <u>a lot of</u> eggs and bacon.
Tom and Betty:	No, thank you, Aunt Betty. A roll and a cup of tea or coffee — that's enough. We Austrians don't eat so <u>much</u> for breakfast!

Beachte!

MUCH .... "viel" ⎫ die Menge ist
LITTLE ..... "wenig" ⎭ **nicht zählbar**

MANY .... "viele" ⎫ die bezeichneten Gegen-
FEW .... "wenige" ⎭ stände können **einzeln gezählt werden**

Anmerkung!
Anstelle von "MUCH", "MANY" verwendet man oft "A LOT OF".
"MUCH, "MANY" werden vorwiegend in **Frage und Verneinung** verwendet.

1. *Lies den Dialog im Kästchen gut durch und beachte jeweils "MUCH, MANY, LITTLE, FEW"!*

2. *Bilde Sätze nach folgendem Muster!*

> Oh, I'm sorry, there are only a few rolls left.
> I didn't buy many rolls yesterday.

Verwende: apples, oranges, peaches, apricots, . . .

3. *Bilde Sätze nach folgendem Muster!*

> There is not much porridge left.
> Just a little porridge is in the kitchen.

Verwende: bacon, jam, juice, milk, . . .

4. *Setze ein*: a) much (a lot of) - many
   b) little - a few

. . . eggs, . . . water, . . . wine, ...bottles of wine, . . . cups of tea, . . . bread, . . . loaves of bread, . . . juice, . . . bottles of juice, . . . glasses of water, . . . coffee, . . . cups of coffee, . . . ham, . . . slices of ham, . . .

5. *Versuche folgendes Gespräch auf Englisch!*

Aunt Mary: bietet Kaffee an
Betty: sagt, sie hätte gerne etwas Kaffee - wenig nur

Aunt Mary: bietet ein Stück Kuchen an
Tom: lehnt dankend ab

Aunt Mary: bietet Brot und Semmeln an
Tom: sagt, er hätte gerne eine Semmel

Uncle Fred: Waiter, the menu, please!
Waiter: Here's the menu, sir!

The Black Horse Today's Menu	**Main Courses:**
Starters:	Roast mutton with chips and lettuce .... £ 3.95
Turtle Soup .... 95 p	Beefsteak with chips and tomatoes .... £ 3.95
Oxtail Soup .... 95 p	Roast pork with vegetables .... £ 3.95
Vegetable Soup .... 95 p	
Soup of the Day .... 95 p	**Sweets:**
	Ice-cream .... 95 p
	Fruit tart .... 95 p

Betty: Look, Uncle Fred! Every soup is 95p:
turtle soup 95p, oxtail soup 95p, ...

Uncle Fred: Oh no, not every soup, but <u>each of</u> these
starters here is 95p.

Betty: And look at the main courses!
<u>Every</u> main course is £ 3.95!

Uncle Fred: Oh yes, <u>each of</u> these main courses is £ 3.95.
Let's order turtle soup and beefsteak!

Beachte!

EVERY ... jeder(e, s) **allgemein**
EACH ... jeder(e, s) auf eine **bestimmte** Gruppe von
Personen / Dingen bezogen.

1. Bilde Minidialoge nach folgendem Muster!

> A: Are all these soups here fine?
> B: Yes, each of these soups here is fine.

a) main courses / marvellous
b) cakes / excellent
c) vegetables / fine
d) fruit tarts / sweet

2. Bilde Sätze nach folgendem Muster!

> Every house has a roof.
> Each of these houses has a balcony.

a) cat . . .tail / cats . . . long ears
b) house . . . door / houses . . . 20 windows
c) elephant . . . big ears / elephants . . . a long tail
d) Englishman . . . umbrella / Englishmen . . . black umbrella

3. Setze ein: EVERY oder EACH (OF)!

a) . . . monkey has a long tail.
b) . . . monkey here has a very long tail.
c) . . . house has a chimney.
d) . . . these houses has two chimneys.
e) . . . these men is a teacher.
f) . . . these women here is a shop-assistant.
g) . . . Englishman is polite.
h) . . . these men here is impolite.

4. Versuche folgendes Gespräch auf Englisch!

Uncle Fred: verlangt die Speisekarte
Betty: stellt mit Erstaunen fest, daß jede dieser Suppen 95p kostet
Uncle Fred: meint, das sei lustig, und zeigt Betty, daß jede der Hauptspeisen £ 3.95 kostet

A. Streiche den Buchstaben vor dem Wort durch, das in die Lücke paßt!

> Tom was ill. He . . . not do his homework.

    a) can   ~~b) could~~   c) are able   d) were able

1. Last summer the farmer . . . bring in the hay.
    a) must   b) has to   c) had to   d) have to

2. . . . cross the road when the traffic light is red.
    a) Must   b) Don't   c) Have to   d) Could

3. Wash the pots, please! But you . . . wash the glasses.
    a) need not   b) can   c) had to   d) has to

4. All the children . . . help the farmer.
    a) has to   b) can   c) was able to   d) need

5. You . . . drive on the right side of the road.
    a) must not   b) is able to   c) was able to   d) has to

6. Peter isn't tall enough. He . . . reach the apples.
    a) must   b) isn't able to   c) could   d) have to

7. Joe was very tired. He . . . help in the kitchen.
    a) wasn't able to   b) can   c) weren't able to   d) have to

8. . . . run across the road!
    a) Must not   b) Can   c) Don't   d) Could

                                                    points: | 8 |

B. Ergänze jeweils den fehlenden Satzteil!

If Peter were rich, he *would make* a journey.
                              (to make)

1. If Ann _____ much money, she would buy a house.
    (to have)

2. If the Millers were in Austria, they _____ skiing.
                              (to go)

3. If Pat _____ in London, he would visit Madame Tussaud's.
    (to be)

4. If the children had time, they _____ to the cinema.
                       (to go)   points: | 8 |

C. Setze die fehlenden Vorwörter ein!

1. Who is that woman . . . you? (hinter dir)
2. Mrs Greene. Her husband is . . . me. (neben mir)
3. I haven't been to London . . . 1980. (seit)
4. Tom isn't . . . school. (in der Schule)
5. They haven't been to New York . . . years. (seit Jahren)

6. The children aren't . . . home. (zu Hause)
7. This is a book . . . Austria. (über Österreich)
8. I can't find my hat. I must look . . . it. (suchen)
9. Jim has been in Austria . . . 1978. (seit 1978)
10. He has been there . . . 7 years. (seit 7 Jahren)   points: 10

D. Setze ein: a) MUCH (A LOT OF) - MANY

1. There is not . . . porridge left.
2. There are not . . .apples in the basket.
3. There is . . . of jam in the glass.

b) LITTLE - FEW

4. There is only a . . . milk in the glass.
5. There were only a . . . boys in the classroom.
6. There are a . . . animals in the zoo.   points: 6

E. Setze ein: EVERY - EACH (OF)

1. . . . cat has 2 ears.
2. . . . these cats has long ears.
3. . . . these houses has a balcony.
4. . . . house has a roof.
5. . . . Englishman has an umbrella.
6. . . . these Englishmen has two umbrellas.   points: 6

*F. Das folgende Gespräch soll nicht wörtlich, sondern nur sinngemäß
wiedergegeben werden! (pro Satz 2 Punkte)*

Tom macht den Vorschlag, eine Party zu geben!	*Let's have a party!*
1. Jim meint, das sei eine gute Idee.	
2. Tom sagt, sie könnten alle Freunde einladen.	
3. Jim meint, sie könnten einen Kuchen zubereiten.	
4. Tom sagt, daß sie das tun wollen.	

points: 8

A. - F.:   46

	very good	more revision needed
AHS, LG1	38 points and more	not even 32 points
LG 2	34 points and more	not even 28 points
LG 3	30 points and more	not even 24 points

137

1 PEN FRIENDS ALL OVER THE WORLD

1. a) Jane wants an Austrian pen friend.
    b) Betty wants an Australian pen friend.
    c) She lives in Canada.
    d) He is 12 years old.
    e) No, they don't. They live in Italy.
    f) Sue's hobbies are singing and travelling.

2. a) **James** is thirteen years old.
       He lives in Australia.
       His hobbies are reading books and writing letters.

    b) **Hans** is twelve years old.
       He lives in Austria.
       His hobbies are music and animals.

    c) **Sue** is thirteen years old.
       She lives in Ireland.
       Her hobbies are singing and travelling.

    d) **Anna and Maria** are thirteen years old.
       They live in Italy.
       Their hobbies are taking photos and swimming.

3. a) **Tom** wants to write a letter. **He** writes a letter to Mary. Mary is **his** pen friend.
    b) **Jim and I** want to have pen friends in Italy, so **we** write to Anna and Maria. Anna and Maria are **our** pen friends.
    c) **Ann and Joe** are going to write a card to James. So **they** are going to write to Australia.
    d) **Nelly** wants an Irish pen friend. **She** is going to write to Sue.
    e) **Nelly's** pen friend is Sue. **Her** pen friend lives in Ireland.
    f) **Peter's** pen friend is 13 years old. **His** pen friend lives in England.
    g) **Susan's** pen friend is 12 years old. **Her** pen friend lives in Austria.

4. Keine Angaben möglich; individuelle Lösungsmöglichkeiten!

2. a) Yes, I have.
   b) No, he hasn't.
   c) Yes, they have.
   d) No, I haven't.
   e) Yes, she has.
   f) Yes, they have.

3. a) Yes, they are.
   b) No, he isn't.
   c) Yes, I am.
   d) Yes, they are.
   e) No, she isn't.
   f) Yes, I am.

4. a) Yes, I do.
   b) No, he doesn't.
   c) No, she didn't.
   d) Yes, they do.
   e) No, he didn't.
   f) Yes, she does.

5. a) Yes, I am. / No, I'm not.
   b) Yes, I do. / No, I don't.
   c) Yes, I can. / No, I can't.
   d) Yes, he (she) does. / No, he (she) doesn't.
   e) Yes, I have. / No, I haven't.
   f) Yes, I do. / No, I don't.
   g) Yes, he (she) is. / No, he (she) isn't.
   h) Yes, he (she) has. / No, he (she) hasn't.
   i) Yes, I did. / No, I didn't.
   j) Yes, I did. / No, I didn't.
   k) Yes, he (she) can. / No, he (she) can't.
   l) Yes, I am. / No, I'm not.

3 WHERE ARE ALL MY SCHOOL THINGS?

1. This fountain-pen here belongs to me, that fountain-pen over there belongs to you.

   This ruler here belongs to me, that ruler over there belongs to you.

   This satchel here belongs to me, that satchel over there belongs to you.

This pencil-case here belongs to me, that pencil-case over there belongs to you.

This copy-book here belongs to me, that copy-book over there belongs to you.

2. These fountain-pens here belong to me, those fountain-pens over there belong to you.

These rulers here belong to me, those rulers over there belong to you.

These satchels here belong to me, those satchels over there belong to you.

These pencil-cases here belong to me, those pencil-cases over there belong to you.

These copy-books here belong to me, those copy-books over there belong to you.

3. Mum: What about these ball-pens here?
   Sue: I think these ball-pens belong to Jack, those ball-pens over there belong to me.

   Mum: What about these books here?
   Sue: I think these books belong to Jack, those books over there belong to me.

   Mum: What about these rubbers here?
   Sue: I think these rubbers belong to Jack, those rubbers over there belong to me.

   Mum: What about these pencil-sharpeners here?
   Sue: I think these pencil-sharpeners belong to Jack, those pencil-sharpeners over there belong to me.

   Mum: What about these triangles here?
   Sue: I think these triangles belong to Jack, those triangles over there belong to me.

4. A: This ruler belongs to me.
   B: That over there is your ruler.

   A: This pencil-sharpener belongs to me.
   B: That over there is your pencil-sharpener.

   A: These books belong to me.
   B: Those over there are your books.

A: These pencils belong to me.
B: Those over there are your pencils.

A: These copy-books belong to me.
B: Those over there are your copy-books.

5. a) **This** satchel here belongs to me.
   b) **Those** books over there are Tom's.
   c) **These** pencils here are Betty's.
   d) What about **this** exercise-book here?
   e) I think **these** rulers here are Jim's.
   f) And what about **those** rulers over there?

EVERYONE IS BUSY!

1. a) **I'm writing** a letter **just now.**
      I always write a letter in the evening.

   b) **I'm playing** football **just now.**
      I always play football in the afternoon.

   c) **I'm drinking** tea **just now.**
      I always drink tea in the morning.

   d) **I'm eating** a piece of cake **just now.**
      I always eat a piece of cake in the afternoon.

2. a) **Tom is writing** a letter **just now.**
      He always writes a letter in the evening.

   b) **Tom is playing** football **just now.**
      He always plays football in the afternoon.

   c) **Tom is drinking** tea **just now.**
      He always drinks tea in the morning.

   d) **Tom is eating** a piece of cake **just now.**
      He always eats a piece of cake in the afternoon.

3. a) Sue: This is Sue speaking.
      Joe: Hello, Sue! What are you doing?
      Sue: I'm just learning French. I always learn French in the
           afternoon.
      Joe: I'm just studying mathematics. I always study mathematics
           on Wednesday afternoon.
           And what is your sister Betty doing?

141

Sue: She is going for a walk at the moment. She often goes for a walk in the afternoon.

Joe: It's a pity that everone is busy. I'm afraid we can't go out this afternoon. Bye, bye!

Sue: Good-bye, Joe!

b) Jack: This is Jack speaking.

John: Hello, Jack! What are you doing?

Jack: I'm just reading a book. I always read a book in the afternoon.

John: I'm just making my bed. I always make my bed on Wednesday afternoon.
And what is your brother Pat doing?

Jack: He is doing his homework at the moment. He often does his homework in the afternoon.

John: It's a pity that everyone is busy. I'm afraid we can't go out this afternoon! Bye, bye!

Jack: Good-bye, John!

4. .a) Look! The boys **are running!**
They **run** to school every morning.

b) Listen! Betty **is singing** an American song.
She often **sings** American songs.

c) Ann and Pat always **dance** in the evening.
Look! They **are dancing** just now.

d) Peter often **eats** an apple.
Yes, he **is eating** an apple again.

5 TEA-TIME

1. a) I like bread but **I don't like** cakes.
   b) I like jelly but **I don't like** porridge.
   c) I like cornflakes but **I don't like** biscuits.
   d) I like juice but **I don't like** beer.
   e) I like milk but **I don't like** wine.
   f) I like cocoa but **I don't like** whisky.

2. I don't want to go to school.
   I don't want to help in the kitchen.
   I don't want to eat ice-cream.
   I don't want to go to the cinema.

Peter doesn't want to go to school.
Peter doesn't want to help in the kitchen.
Peter doesn't want to eat ice-cream.
Peter doesn't want to go to the cinema.

Sue and Ellen don't want to go to school.
Sue and Ellen don't want to help in the kitchen.
Sue and Ellen don't want to eat ice-cream.
Sue and Ellen don't want to go to the cinema.

Mary doesn't want to go to school.
Mary doesn't want to help in the kitchen.
Mary doesn't want to eat ice-cream.
Mary doesn't want to go to the cinema.

3. a) A: Does your sister eat rolls?
      B: Of course, she does!
         But she doesn't eat bread.

   b) A: Does your girl friend drink coffee?
      B: Of course, she does!
         But she doesn't drink cocoa.

   c) A: Does your father like beer?
      B: Of course, he does!
         But he doesn't like wine.

   d) A: Does your mother eat cakes?
      B: Of course, she does!
         But she doesn't eat biscuits.

4. a) No, I don't.
   b) Yes, she does.
   c) No, I don't.
   d) No, they don't
   e) No, they don't.
   f) No, he doesn't.
   g) Yes, he does.
   h) No, they don't.

5. Keine Angaben möglich; individuelle Lösungsmöglichkeiten!

6 LITTLE SUSY ALWAYS ASKS QUESTIONS

1 a) Who is in the garden?
   b) Who can sing English songs?
   c) Who reads German books?
   d) Who plays in the garden?
   e) Who asks the teacher?
   f) Who learns English?
   g) Who is at school?
   h) Who can swim?

2. a) Where is Peter?
   b) Where does Jane play?
   c) Where does Pat run to?
   d) Where can Sandy go to?
   e) Where is Joe?
   f) Where does Sue go to?
   g) Where does Mary help?
   h) Where does Ann write her exercises?

3. a) When can Peter go?
   b) When does Jane go to school?
   c) When does Pat come home?
   d) When does Sandy do her exercises?
   e) When is Joe at home?
   f) When may Sue leave?
   g) When does Mary read her books?
   h) When does Ann work?

4. a) When can Dad come, Mum?
   b) What is Dad writing, Mum?
   c) Where is my ball, Mum?
   d) Where can I play, Mum?
   e) When can I play in the garden, Mum?
   f) Where are you working, Mum?

7 WHAT WE DID LAST SUMMER

1. When the weather was fine I went swimming.
   When the weather was fine I played outdoor games.
   When the weather was bad I watched TV.
   When the weather was bad I wrote postcards.

   When the weather was fine Tom went swimming.
   When the weather was fine Tom played outdoor games.

When the weather was bad Tom watched TV.
When the weather was bad Tom wrote postcards.

When the weather was fine Sue went swimming.
When the weather was fine Sue played outdoor games.
When the weather was bad Sue watched TV.
When the weather was bad Sue wrote postcards.

2. a) Ann liked playing tennis best, so she often played tennis.
   b) Tom liked climbing mountains best, so he often climbed mountains.
   c) Sue liked picking mushrooms best, so she often picked mushrooms.
   d) Joe and Jack liked riding on horseback best, so they often rode on horseback.
   e) Nelly and Fred liked drinking Coke best, so they often drank Coke.
   f) Sandy liked going to the country best, so she often went to the country.

3. a) Tom: Let's climb mountains!
      Pat: Oh no, we climbed mountains yesterday!

   b) Tom: Let's play tennis!
      Pat: Oh no, we played tennis yesterday!

   c) Tom: Let's pick mushrooms!
      Pat: Oh no, we picked mushrooms yesterday!

   d) Tom: Let's drink Coke!
      Pat: Oh no, we drank Coke yesterday!

   e) Tom: Let's ride on horseback!
      Pat: Oh no, we rode on horseback yesterday!

   f) Tom: Let's go to the country!
      Pat: Oh no, we went to the country yesterday!

4. a) I spent my summer holidays in the country (in town, at the seaside).
   b) I stayed with my parents (with my friends . . .).
   c) I stayed for . . . weeks (months, . . .).
   d) When the weather was bad I went sightseeing.
   e) When the weather was fine I went swimming.
   f) I liked swimming (boating, climbing, . . .) best.
   g) I saw a castle (a museum, many ships, . . .)
   h) I returned home on the . . . of . . . .

5. Individuelle Lösungsmöglichkeiten!

145

8 LAST SUMMER — EVERY SUMMER

2. a) A: Did you go sightseeing last summer?
   B: Yes, I went sightseeing. I usually go sightseeing in summer.

   b) A: Did you read books last summer?
   B: Yes, I read books. I usually read books in summer.

   c) A: Did you eat ice-cream last summer?
   B: Yes, I ate ice-cream. I usually eat ice-cream in summer.

   d) A: Did you travel to Austria last summer?
   B: Yes, I travelled to Austria. I usually travel to Austria in summer.

   e) A: Did you pick flowers last summer?
   B: Yes, I picked flowers last summer. I usually pick flowers in summer.

3. Last summer Tom **played** tennis.
   He often **plays** tennis when the weather is fine.

   Jim **writes** his exercises in the afternoon.
   Yesterday he **wrote** his exercises in the evening.

   Every Tuesday Peter **goes** swimming.
   Yesterday was Tuesday: he **went** swimming.

   On Monday Ann **comes** home at 4.
   Yesterday was Monday, so she **came** home at 4.

   Last month Tom **read** three books.
   He often **reads** books in the evening.

   Yesterday I **ate** five apples.
   In summer I **eat** many apples.

4. a) Fred did not write Joe's full address.
   b) Because Fred forgot to write Joe's full address.
   c) Yes, I did. / No, I didn't.

A. 1. c)
   2. a)
   3. d)
   4. a)
   5. d)
   6. d)
   7. d)
   8. b)
   9. c)
   10. a)
   11. b)
   12. c)

B. 1. Yes, I can.
   2. No, they aren't.
   3. Yes, I am.
   4. Yes, I do.
   5. Yes, she does.
   6. Yes, I have.
   7. No, he hasn't.
   8. Yes, he did.

C. 1. Where . . .
   2. What . . .
   3. When . . .
   4. Who . . .
   5. Who . . .
   6. When . . .

D. 1. doesn't
   2. don't
   3. don't
   4. don't
   5. don't
   6. doesn't

E. 1. her / it
   2. their / They
   3. his / He
   4. you / I
   5. them / They

9 HOLIDAY WEATHER

1. 2 Austria
    9 France
   10 Germany
    1 Great Britain
    4 Greece
    7 Hungary
   11 Italy
   13 Ireland
   12 Portugal
    8 Spain
    3 Switzerland
    5 Turkey
    6 Yugoslavia

2. a) Teacher: Where did you spend your holidays, Joe?
      Joe: I spent my holidays in France.
                 It was cloudy but quite nice.
                 The temperatures were about 22 degrees.

   b) Teacher: Where did you spend your holidays, Nelly?
      Nelly: I spent my holidays in Austria.
                 Is was sunny and very warm.
                 The temperatures were about 28 degrees.

   c) Teacher: Where did you spend your holidays, Peter?
      Peter: I spent my holidays in Italy.
                 It was sunny and hot.
                 The temperatures were about 32 degrees.

   d) Teacher: Where did you spend your holidays, Riza?
      Riza: I spent my holidays in Turkey.
                 It was sunny and very hot.
                 The temperatures were about 35 degrees.

   e) Teacher: Where did you spend your holidays, Anica?
      Anica: I spent my holidays in Yugoslavia.
                 It was cloudy but quite warm.
                 The temperatures were about 29 degrees.

3. 2 Paris   1 Vienna   7 Rome
    6 London   3 Bonn   10 Madrid
    4 Athens   12 Ankara   13 Belgrade
    5 Budapest   8 Dublin   9 Lisbon
                   11 Berne

4. Paris is the capital of France.
   London is the capital of Great Britain.
   Athens is the capital of Greece.
   Budapest is the capital of Hungary.
   Bonn is the capital of Germany.
   Rome is the capital of Italy.
   Dublin is the capital of Ireland.
   Lisbon is the capital of Portugal.
   Madrid is the capital of Spain.
   Berne is the capital of Switzerland.
   Ankara is the capital of Turkey.
   Belgrade is the capital of Yugoslavia.

5. a) Sue: I was in France.
      Joe: And did you see Paris?
      Sue: Yes, we were in Paris, too.

   b) Nelly: I was in Austria.
      Joe: And did you see Vienna?
      Nelly: Yes, we were in Vienna, too.

   c) Peter: I was in Italy.
      Joe: And did you see Rome?
      Peter: Yes, we were in Rome, too.

   d) Riza: I was in Turkey.
      Joe: And did you see Ankara?
      Riza: Yes, we were in Ankara, too.

   e) Anica: I was in Yugoslavia.
      Joe: And did you see Belgrade?
      Anica: Yes, we were in Belgrade, too.

   f) Jane: I was in Great Britain.
      Joe: And did you see London?
      Jane: Yes, we were in London, too.

6. A: What was the weather like in Budapest on the fifteenth of
      September?
   B: It was cloudy. The temperatures were about 15° C.

   A: What was the weather like in Dublin on the fifteenth of
      September?
   B: It was rainy. The temperatures were about 12° C.

   A: What was the weather like in London on the fifteenth of
      September?
   B: It was rainy. The temperatures were about 11° C.

A: What was the weather like in Madrid on the fifteenth of September?
B: It was sunny. The temperatures were about 25° C.

A: What was the weather like in Paris on the fifteenth of September?
B: It was cloudy. The temperatures were about 18° C.

A: What was the weather like in Rome on the fifteenth of September?
B: It was sunny. The temperatures were about 26° C.

A: What was the weather like in Vienna on the fifteenth of September?
B: It was sunny. The temperatures were about 21° C.

10 JUMBLED SENTENCES

1. Richtige Reihenfolge: 1, 6, 5, 3, 2, 4.

2. were — to be
   travelled — to travel
   was — to be
   arrived — to arrive
   went — to go
   saw — to see

3. Greetings from Greece / Athens!
   The weather is fine, so I can go swimming.
   Yesterday I went to Athens to see the Acropolis.
   Athens is very interesting.
   Give my love to your sister / your parents . . .

4. Individuelle Lösungsmöglichkeiten!

5. Eine von vielen Lösungsmöglichkeiten:
   Betty: Hello, Ann! This is Betty speaking!
   Ann: Hello, Betty!
   Betty: Where did you spend your holidays?
   Ann: I spent my holidays in Greece.
   Betty: Did you see the Acropolis in Athens?
   Ann: Yes, of course, I did.
   Betty: What about the weather?
   Ann: Oh, it was lovely, really lovely!
   Betty: When did you come back to London?

Ann: I came back on the third of September.
Betty: I'd like to invite you to tea for tomorrow. I hope you can come.
Ann: That's very nice of you, thank you!

1 HOLIDAY ACTIVITIES

2. a) A: Did you go sightseeing or swimming?
       B: I didn't go sightseeing, I went swimming.

   b) A: Did you play baseball or table-tennis?
       B: I didn't play baseball, I played table-tennis.

   c) A: Did you travel to Italy or to Greece?
       B: I didn't travel to Italy, I travelled to Greece.

   d) A: Did you go by plane or by car?
       B: I didn't go by plane, I went by car.

   e) A: Did you visit Rome or Florence?
       B: I didn't visit Rome, I visited Florence.

   f) A: Did you arrive at Stansted or at Heathrow?
       B: I didn't arrive at Stansted, I arrived at Heathrow.

3. The children didn't learn English during the holidays.
   The children didn't write exercises during the holidays.
   The children didn't play on the piano during the holidays.
   The children didn't help Mum during the holidays.
   The children didn't clean their rooms during the holidays.
   The children didn't work in the garden during the holidays.

4. a) Little Joe didn't go to Regent's Park.
   b) Little Joe didn't cross Oxford Street.
   c) Little Joe didn't buy fine things.
   d) Little Joe didn't see Tower Bridge.
   e) Little Joe didn't take a photo of the Houses of Parliament.
   f) Little Joe didn't hear Big Ben.

5. He **went** to London but he **didn't go** to Oxford.
   He **wrote** letters but he **didn't write** postcards.
   We **read** books but we **didn't read** the newspaper.
   She **sang** English songs but she **didn't sing** Austrian songs.
   She **took** her umbrella but she **didn't take** her raincoat.

12 YOU CAN COME, CAN'T YOU?

1. a) Peter is a good boy, **isn't he?**
   b) Joe wasn't at your party, **was he?**
   c) Betty can read English books, **can't she?**
   d) Ann can't write, **can she?**
   e) The children were at school, **weren't they?**
   f) Tom and Sue weren't at home, **were they?**
   g) The children are in the garden, **aren't they?**
   h) You aren't lazy, **are you?**
   i) Jane hasn't got a new pullover, **has she?**
   j) You have got a lot of work to do, **haven't you?**

2. A: This is my pen, isn't it?
   B: Yes, it is.

   A: This is your pen, isn't it?
   B: Yes, it is.

   A: This is my pullover, isn't it?
   B: Yes, it is.

   A: This is your pullover, isn't it?
   B: Yes, it is.

   A: These are my books, aren't they?
   B: Yes, they are.

   A: These are your books, aren't they?
   B: Yes, they are.

   A: These are my shoes, aren't they?
   B: Yes, they are.

   A: These are your shoes, aren't they?
   B: Yes, they are.

3. a) It's not going to rain, **is it?** No, it is not.
   b) Yesterday was very cold, **wasn't it?** Yes, it was.
   c) Last month was very wet, **wasn't it?** Yes, it was.
   d) It's really a fine day, **isn't it?** Yes, it is.

4. a) Is Jane a good girl?
      No, she isn't, is she?

b) Was Peter in the garden?
   No, he wasn't, was he?

c) Has Pat got a new bag?
   No, he hasn't, has he?

d) Were the children at school?
   No, they weren't, were they?

TITTLE-TATTLE

1. a) Mrs Miller bought a car, **didn't she?**
   b) Mr Miller comes home at 10, **doesn't he?**
   c) Mrs Miller buys everything in Regent Street, **doesn't she?**
   d) Mrs Miller wore a new fur-coat, **didn't she?**
   e) Mr Miller runs a big shop, **doesn't he?**
   f) The Millers don't work in summer, **do they?**
   g) Mrs Miller didn't help her husband, **did she?**

2. A: This pullover belongs to you, doesn't it?
   B: Yes, it does.

   A: This pen belongs to you, doesn't it?
   B: Yes, it does.

   A: These shoes belong to you, don't they?
   B: Yes, they do.

   A: These books belong to you, don't they?
   B: Yes, they do.

3. a) Does Mrs Miller do the shopping?
      Yes, she does, doesn't she?

   b) Does Mr Miller wash his car?
      Yes, he does, doesn't he?

   c) Does Mr Miller work in the garden?
      Yes, he does, doesn't he?

   d) Does Mrs Miller like swimming?
      Yes, she does, doesn't she?

4. a) Do the Millers travel to Austria in winter?
      No, they don't, do they?

b) Do the Millers fly to Greece in summer?
No, they don't, do they?

c) Do the Millers go to the theatre?
No, they don't, do they?

d) Do the Millers watch TV?
No, they don't, do they?

14 WHY NOT? ... BECAUSE ...

1. Sue can't go to the cinema because she's got to do her homework.
Jane wants to buy some presents because it's Christmas.
Peter can't play in the garden because it's too cold today.
Pat is late for school because he missed the bus.

2. a) Tom would like to speak to Jim because he wants to play tennis with him.
   b) He can't do his homework because he is too tired.
   c) Ann wants to drink tea because she is thirsty.
   d) Betty wants to eat an apple because she is hungry.
   e) Granny can't play football because she is too old.

3. a) Jim can't play tennis because he is ill.
   b) Jim can't go to school because he is too weak.
   c) Jim can't play the piano because he is too busy.
   d) Jim can't sing a song because he is too hoarse.
   e) Jim can't do his homework because he is too tired.

4. Tom: Hello, Mrs Brown! This is Tom speaking!
   Mrs Brown: Hello, Tom!
   Tom: I'd like to speak to Jim because I want to play tennis with him.
   Mrs Brown: Jim can't play tennis. He is ill.
   Tom: Pardon — why not?
   Mrs Brown: He can't play tennis because he is ill. (And so on)

5. Zum Beispiel:
   a) I'm late for school because the alarm-clock didn't work.
   b) My copy-book is not in my satchel because my satchel is too small.
   c) I didn't study the new words because I was ill.
   d) I didn't go to school because I had a sore foot.
   e) I can't help you because I'm too weak.

154

5 DON'T BE SO NOSY!

1. a) Why can't Pat write a letter?
   He can't write a letter because he has no pen.

   b) Why can't Ann eat her breakfast?
   She can't eat her breakfast because she isn't hungry.

   c) Why can't Bert ask the teacher?
   He can't ask the teacher because he is afraid of him.

   d) Why can't Joe go to school?
   He can't go to school because he has a sore foot.

   e) Why can't Betty sing a song?
   She can't sing a song because she has a cold.

2. a) Why does Pat not write a letter?
   He doesn't write a letter because he has no pen.

   b) Why does Ann not eat her breakfast?
   She doesn't eat her breakfast because she isn't hungry.

   c) Why does Bert not ask the teacher?
   He doesn't ask the teacher because he is afraid of him.

   d) Why does Joe not go to school?
   He doesn't go to school because he has a sore foot.

   e) Why does Betty not sing a song?
   She doesn't sing a song because she has a cold.

3. a) Why did Pat not write a letter?
   He didn't write a letter because he had no pen.

   b) Why did Ann not eat her breakfast?
   She didn't eat her breakfast because she wasn't hungry.

   c) Why did Bert not ask the teacher?
   He didn't ask the teacher because he was afraid of him.

   d) Why did Joe not go to school?
   He didn't go to school because he had a sore foot.

   e) Why did Betty not sing a song?
   She didn't sing a song because she had a cold.

4. a) Why can't Jim go to school?
   b) Why don't Tom and Ann like tonic water?
   c) Why can't Jack and Joe write their exercises?

d) Why didn't Peter put on his pullover?
e) Why doesn't Mary take off her coat?
f) Why didn't Joe sing?
g) Why doesn't Nelly do her exercises?
h) Why don't the children play in the garden?

5. Little Jack: Is Peter at home?
   Mother: No, he isn't.
   Little Jack: Why is Peter not at home?
   Mother: He isn't at home because he went swimming.

16 AT THE TRAVEL AGENCY

1. London is interesting.
   London sights are fascinating.
   London cinemas are thrilling.
   Madam Tussaud's is amusing.
   Oxford Street is exciting.

2. a) A: Why do Tom and Betty want to travel to London?
      B: They want to travel to London because London theatres and
         cinemas are thrilling.

   b) A: Why do Tom and Betty want to travel to London?
      B: They want to travel to London because'Madam Tussaud's is
         amusing.

   c) A: Why do Tom and Betty want to travel to London?
      B: They want to travel to London because Oxford Street is
         exciting.

   d) A: Why do Tom and Betty want to travel to London?
      B: They want to travel to London because London is interesting.

3. a) London theatres and cinemas are thrilling - so the children want
      to travel to London.
   b) Madam Tussaud's is amusing - so the children want to travel to
      London.
   c) Oxford Street is exciting - so the children want to travel to
      London.
   d) London is interesting - so the children want to travel to London.

4. a) Why do the children travel to London?
      Well, London theatres and cinemas are thrilling!
      That's why the children travel to London.

156

b) Why do the children travel to London?
   Well, Madam Tussaud's is amusing!
   That's why the children travel to London.

c) Why do the children travel to London?
   Well, Oxford Street is exciting!
   That's why the children travel to London.

d) Why do the children travel to London?
   Well, London is interesting!
   That's why the children travel to London.

5. London taxis are quick. **That's why** many Londoners go by taxi.
   The Underground is quick. **That's why** many Londoners go by Underground.
   London railways are quick. **That's why** many Londoners go by railway.
   The Green Line Buses are quick. **That's why** many Londoners go by Green Line Buses.

7 WHAT CAN WE PLAY THIS AFTERNOON?

1. a) A: Do you really want to go skiing?
      B: We haven't got an anorak and we haven't got sticks - so it's impossible to go skiing.

   b) A: Do you really want to go swimming?
      B: We haven't got a swimming suit and we haven't got a bathing-cap - so it's impossible to go swimming.

   c) A: Do you really want to play cards?
      B: We haven't got cards and we haven't got money - so it's impossible to play cards.

   d) A: Do you really want to play records?
      B: We haven't got records and we haven't got a record-player - so it's impossible to play records.

2. He lives in Newcastle.

5. "TR" stands for "Turkey".
   "H" stands for "Hungary".
   "S" stands for "Sweden".
   "GB" stands for "Great Britain".
   "F" stands for "France".
   "G" stands for "Greece".

6. USA ... United States of America
   SOS ... Save Our Souls
   UK ... United Kingdom
   BBC ... British Broadcasting Corporation
   TV ... Television
   VIP ... Very Important Person

18 AN INTERVIEW AT THE AIRPORT

1. a) No, she didn't.
   b) No, she didn't.
   c) No, she didn't.
   d) Yes, she did.

2. Where did you go to school?
   When did you want to become an actress?
   Why did you want to become an actress?

3. a) Where did you to to school?
   b) Why did you travel to London?
   c) What did you like best in London?
   d) When did you come to London?
   e) Did you arrive yesterday?

4. a) Where did you start your career?
   b) What did you do in New York?
   c) Why did you become an actress?
   d) When did you come to London?

5. a) **Where** did Miss Smily live?
   b) **What** did she like best?
   c) **When** did she come to New York?
   d) **Why** did she come to London?

19 CAN YOU TELL ME THE WAY TO ..., PLEASE?

1. a) Where is the cinema, please?
   b) Can you tell me the way to the cinema, please?
   c) Excuse me, can you tell me the way to the cinema?

   a) Where is the park, please?
   b) Can you tell me the way to the park, please?
   c) Excuse me, can you tell me the way to the park?

a) Where is the theatre, please?
b) Can you tell me the way to the theatre, please?
c) Excuse me, can you tell me the way to the theatre?

a) Where is the restaurant, please?
b) Can you tell me the way to the restaurant, please?
c) Excuse me, can you tell me the way to the restaurant?

a) Where is the hospital, please?
b) Can you tell me the way to the hospital, please?
c) Excuse me, can you tell me the way to the hospital?

a) Where is the town hall, please?
b) Can you tell me the way to the town hall, please?
c) Excuse me, can you tell me the way to the town hall?

2. a) Go straight on! / Walk straight on!
   b) Cross Park Street!
   c) Walk as far as the traffic-light!
   d) Cross the zebra crossing!

3. a) Turn round!
   b) Take the second on the left!
   c) Take the third on the right!
   d) Go as far as the traffic-light, then turn right!
   e) Go as far as the zebra crossing, then turn left!

4. Excuse me, can you tell me the way to St. Paul's Cathedral, please?
   Excuse me, can you tell me the way to Buckingham Palace, please?
   Excuse me, can you tell me the way to Tower Bridge, please?
   Excuse me, can you tell me the way to Trafalgar Square, please?

5. Individuelle Lösungsmöglichkeiten!

HOW DO YOU GET TO SCHOOL?

1. a) No, she doesn't. She usually goes by bus.
   b) Yes, she usually goes by bus.
   c) No, she doesn't. She sometimes goes by car.
   d) Yes, she sometimes goes by car.

e) No, he doesn't. He always walks on foot.
f) He always walks on foot.
g) I usually go by tram / by bus, . . .

2. a) I **usually** go to school by bike.
   b) The Millers **often** travel to England in summer.
   c) Pat **always** does his work in the afternoon.
   d) I have **always** got a lot of homework.
   e) I **sometimes** play tennis in the afternoon.

3. a) A: How does Mrs Brown usually get to her shop?
        By train?
     B: No, she always gets to her shop by tram.

   b) A: How do the Coopers usually get to Greece?
        By car?
     B: No, they always get to Greece by plane.

   c) A: How does Mr White usually get to the mountains?
        By bus?
     B: No, he always gets to the mountains by helicopter.

   d) A: How do the Millers usually get to Italy?
        By train?
     B: No, they always get to Italy by plane.

4. A: Does Tom always go by bike?
   B: No, he doesn't. He usually walks on foot. He sometimes goes
      by Underground.

21 HOW LONG DOES IT TAKE YOU . . . ?

2. a) It takes me . . . to go to school.
   b) It takes her . . . to prepare dinner.
   c) It takes him . . . to study English.
   d) It takes them . . . to do their homework.
   e) It takes us . . . to write a test.

3. a) A: How long did it take Tom to travel to London?
     B: It took him two hours to travel to London.

   b) A: How long did it take Ann to water the flowers?
     B: It took her five minutes to water the flowers.

   c) A: How long did it take the Coopers to dig the garden?
     B: It took them three hours to dig the garden.

d) A: How long did it take the Smiths to paint the house?
   B: It took them one day to paint the house.

4. a) A: Excuse me, sir, how long does it take me to get to Buckingham Palace?
      B: Go by bus! Then it takes you ten minutes.

   b) A: Excuse me, sir, how long does it take me to get to Trafalgar Square?
      B: Go by Underground! Then it takes you five minutes.

   c) A: Excuse me, sir, how long does it take me to get to Tower Bridge?
      B: Go by boat! Then it takes you twenty minutes.

   d) A: Excuse me, sir, how long does it take me to get to St. Paul's Cathedral?
      B: Go by bus! Then it takes you three minutes.

5. a) How long does it take you to do your homework?
   b) How long does it take you to go to school?
   c) How long does it take you to eat your breakfast?

TRY THIS TEST   UNIT 9 - 21

A.   1. c)
      2. d)
      3. a)
      4. d)
      5. b)
      6. c)
      7. b)
      8. a)
      9. c)
     10. b)
     11. d)
     12. d)

B. 1. didn't go
   2. doesn't play
   3. don't like
   4. didn't ask
   5. didn't see
   6. doesn't read
   7. don't like
   8. didn't take

C. 1. . . . can he?
   2. . . . wasn't she?
   3. . . . didn't they?
   4. . . . did they?
   5. . . . doesn't he?
   6. . . . don't they?

D. 1. What did Pat read?
   2. When did she arrive?
   3. Where did the children play?
   4. Why did she come to London?

E. Walk straight on as far as the traffic-light.
   How long does it take me to get to Tower Bridge?
   Take the bus! Then it takes you five minutes to get to Tower Bridge.
   Thank you!

F. 1. Tom sometimes plays in the garden.
   2. We often go to London by car.
   3. I always do my exercises in the morning.
   4. I always play tennis in the afternoon.

22 AS COLD AS . . . AS HOT AS . . . AS WARM AS . . .

1. a) A: It's cool in Copenhagen, isn't it?
         What do you think? Is it cool in Moscow, too?
      B: Let's have a look into the newspaper!
      A: Oh, in Moscow it's just **as cold as** in Copenhagen.
         And what about Oslo?
      B: In Oslo it's just **as cold as** in Moscow.
      A: Let's travel to Cairo!

   b) A: It's warm in Vienna, isn't it?
         What do you think? Is it warm in Berlin, too?
      B: Let's have a look into the newspaper!
      A: Oh, in Berlin it's just **as warm as** in Vienna.
         And what about Paris?
      B: In Paris it's just **as warm as** in Berlin.
      A: Let's travel to Copenhagen!

   c) A: It's hot in Athens, isn't it?
         What do you think? Is it hot in Rome, too?
      B: Let's have a look into the newspaper!

A: Oh, in Rome it's just **as hot as** in Athens.
   And what about Madrid?
B: In Madrid it's just **as hot as** in Rome.
A: Let's travel to Vienna!

2. 6 the wind
    1 fire
    5 the sun
    2 the night
    4 snow
    3 Rome
    8 stone
    9 ice
    7 the sky
   12 diamonds
   11 a knife
   10 coffee

3. as dark as the night
   as old as Rome
   as white as snow
   as bright as the sun
   as strong as the wind
   as blue as the sky
   as hard as stone
   as cold as ice
   as bitter as coffee
   as sharp as a knife
   as prescious as diamonds

4. a) No, a boy isn't **as big as** a man.
   b) No, a house isn't **as high as** a mountain.
   c) No, water isn't **as cold as** ice.
   d) No, beer isn't **as strong as** wine.
   e) No, the English test isn't **as difficult as** the maths test.
   f) No, he isn't **as old as** his father.

5. a) A: This exercise is difficult. This test is difficult, too.
      B: Look! The exercise is just **as difficult as** the test.

   b) A: This house is high. This tree is high, too.
      B: Look! The house is just **as high as** the tree.

   c) A: This dress is expensive. This suit is expensive, too.
      B: Look! The dress is just **as expensive as** the suit.

d) A: Mary is beautiful. Susan is beautiful, too.
   B: Look! Mary is just **as beautiful as** Susan.

e) A: Gin is strong. Rum is strong, too.
   B: Look! Gin is just **as strong as** rum.

f) A: Mr Miller is old. Mrs Miller is old, too.
   B: Look! Mr Miller is just **as old as** Mrs Miller.

g) A: This tea is hot. This coffee is hot, too.
   B: Look! The tea is just **as hot as** the coffee.

h) A: London is interesting. Rome is interesting, too.
   B: Look! London is just **as interesting as** Rome.

23 WINDOW-SHOPPING

1. a) long - long**er** - long**est**
   b) strong - strong**er** - strong**est**
   c) short - short**er** - short**est**
   d) high - high**er** - high**est**
   e) happy - happ**ier** - happ**iest**
   f) funny - funn**ier** - funn**iest**
   g) sunny - sunn**ier** - sunn**iest**
   h) heavy - heav**ier** - heav**iest**
   i) interesting - **more** interesting - **most** interesting
   j) expensive - **more** expensive - **most** expensive
   k) beautiful - **more** beautiful - **most** beautiful
   l) wonderful - **more** wonderful - **most** wonderful

2. a) A pig is big.
      A cow is bigg**er**.
      An elephant is bigg**est**.

   b) Mary is beautiful.
      Ann is **more** beautiful.
      Nelly is **most** beautiful.

   c) A handbag is heavy.
      A rucksack is heav**ier**.
      A suitcase is heav**iest**.

   d) A Mini is expensive.
      A Jaguar is **more** expensive.
      A Rolls Royce is **most** expensive.

e) An English test is easy.
   A French test is easi**er**.
   A maths test is easi**est**.

f) London is interesting.
   Vienna is **more** interesting.
   Rome is **most** interesting.

3. a) A: I'm looking for a new jacket.
      B: Look! There are three jackets in that shop-window!
      A: Oh, yes, the blue jacket is cheap.
      B: And look! The white jacket is even cheaper.
      . . . and the red jacket is the cheapest.

   b) A: I'm looking for a new dress.
      B: Look! There are three dresses in that shop-window!
      A: Oh, yes, the green dress is nice.
      B: And look! The red dress is even nicer . . . and the white dress is
         the nicest.

   c) A: I'm looking for a new coat.
      B: Look! There are three coats in that shop-window!
      A: Oh, yes, the brown coat is expensive.
      B: And look! The black coat is even more expensive . . . and the
         red coat is the most expensive.

   d) A: I'm looking for a new pullover.
      B: Look! There are three pullovers in that shop-window!
      A: Oh, yes, the pink pullover is beautiful.
      B: And look! The blue pullover is even more beautiful . . . and the
         grey pullover is the most beautiful.

4. Is it cheaper to eat fish or steaks?
   It's cheaper to eat fish.

   Is it cheaper to eat bread or sandwiches?
   It's cheaper to eat bread.

   Is it more expensive to eat fish or steaks?
   It's more expensive to eat steaks.

   Is it more expensive to eat bread or sandwiches?
   It's more expensive to eat sandwiches.

   Is it cheaper to drink wine or whisky?
   It's cheaper to drink wine.

   Is it cheaper to drink Cola or water?
   It's cheaper to drink water.

165

Is it more expensive to drink wine or whisky?
It's more expensive to drink whisky.

Is it more expensive to drink Cola or water?
It's more expensive to drink Cola.

24 TALKING ABOUT THE WEATHER

1. worse: schlechter
   less: weniger
   better: besser
   more: mehr

2. a) No   b) Yes   c) No   d) No   e) No   f) Yes   g) No

3. a) Today's dinner was bad.
      Yesterday it was even worse.

   b) Today's TV programme is bad.
      Yesterday it was even worse.

   c) Today's football match was bad.
      Yesterday it was even worse.

   d) Today's news are very bad.
      Yesterday they were even worse.

4. It's better to eat less chocolate.
   It's better to drink less wine.
   It's better to drink less black coffee.
   It's better to drink more milk.
   It's better to drink more juice.
   It's better to eat more vegetables.

5. a) When it is hot it's the best thing to take off one's pullover.
   b) When you are hungry it's the best thing to eat some bread.
   c) When you are tired it's the best thing to go to bed.
   d) When you are thirsty it's the best thing to drink some water.

25 I AM STRONGER THAN YOU!

1. a) Ann: I'm more beautiful than you!
      Betty: No, you are not!
               I am more beautiful than you!
      Mother: Don't quarrel!
               Ann is just as beautiful as Betty!

b) Peter: I'm cleverer than you!
   Jim: No, you are not!
   I am cleverer than you!
   Father: Don't quarrel!
   Peter is just as clever as Jim!

c) Jane: I'm more intelligent than you!
   Susan: No, you are not!
   I am more intelligent than you!
   Mother: Don't quarrel!
   Jane is just as intelligent as Susan!

d) Pat: I'm quicker than you!
   Joe: No, you are not!
   I am quicker than you!
   Father: Don't quarrel!
   Pat is just as quick as Joe!

2. a) Ann is more beautiful than Mary.
   Nelly is more beautiful than Ann.

   b) A cow is bigger than a pig.
   An elephant is bigger than a cow.

   c) A rucksack is heavier than a handbag.
   A suitcase is heavier than a rucksack.

   d) A Jaguar is more expensive than a Mini.
   A Rolls Royce is more expensive than a Jaguar.

   e) The French test is easier than the English test.
   The maths test is easier than the French test.

3. a) Yesterday it was colder in Athens than in Bangkok.
   b) Yesterday it was colder in Birmingham than in Bristol.
   c) Yesterday it was warmer in Gibraltar than in London.
   d) Yesterday it was warmer in Miami than in Moscow.
   e) Yesterday it was warmer in Rome than in Paris.
   f) Yesterday it was warmer in Sydney than in Tel Aviv.

4. a) No, a house isn't higher than a mountain.
   A mountain is higher than a house.

   b) No, a chair isn't more comfortable than a bed.
   A bed is more comfortable than a chair.

   c) No, boys aren't better pupils than girls.
   Girls are better pupils than boys.

d) No, a village isn't larger than a town.
   A town is larger than a village.

e) No, a bicycle isn't faster than a car.
   A car is faster than a bicycle.

f) No, beer isn't stronger than whisky.
   Whisky is stronger than beer.

g) No, a handbag isn't bigger than a suitcase.
   A suitcase is bigger than a handbag.

h) No, a Rolls Royce isn't cheaper than a Mini.
   A Mini is cheaper than a Rolls Royce.

i) No, a pig isn't bigger than an elephant.
   An elephant is bigger than a pig.

26 WHAT DO THE WEATHERMEN SAY?

1. a) No b) Yes c) Yes d) No e) Yes f) No g) No h) Yes

2. a) No, it isn't.
   b) No, they don't.
   c) The temperature is about 9° C.
   d) The temperature is about 8° C.
   e) The warmest place in Britain was Exeter.
   f) It was coldest in Stornoway.
   g) Yes, it was.
   h) Machrihanish

3. a) It's warmer in London than in Aberdeen.
   b) It's warmer in Cardiff than in Edinburgh.
   c) It's warmer in Bristol than in Belfast.
   d) It's as warm in Newcastle as in Glasgow.

4. a) The sun rises at nine minutes to eight.
   b) The moon rises at seventeen miutes to three.
   c) The moon sets at ten minutes to seven.

27 THE FORTUNE-TELLER
WILL TELL YOU THE FUTURE

1. You will live for a long time.
   You will have 10 children.
   You will get a good job.

You will live in Washington.
You will become a grandmother.

2. We'll be punctual.
We'll get up early.
We'll go to bed in time.
We'll help in the kitchen.
We'll wash our necks.
We'll do our homework.

3. Next summer I shall go swimming.
Next summer I shall travel to New York.
Next summer I shall go sightseeing in London.
Next summer I shall play tennis.

Tomorrow I shall go swimming.
Tomorrow I shall travel to New York.
Tomorrow I shall go sightseeing in London.
Tomorrow I shall play tennis.

Next summer Tom will go swimming.
Next summer Tom will travel to New York.
Next summer Tom will go sightseeing in London.
Next summer Tom will play tennis.

Tomorrow Tom will go swimming.
Tomorrow Tom will travel to New York.
Tomorrow Tom will go sightseeing in London.
Tomorrow Tom will play tennis.

4. Peter won't go to school tomorrow.
Peter won't go skiing tomorrow.
Peter won't go skating tomorrow.

Peter won't go to school next year.
Peter won't go skiing next year.
Peter won't go skating next year.

I shan't go to school tomorrow.
I shan't go skiing tomorrow.
I shan't go skating tomorrow.

I shan't go to school next year.
I shan't go skiing next year.
I shan't go skating next year.

5. It **will be** fine tomorrow. There **will be** no clouds in the sky. It **will be** warm and sunny. It **will be** warmer than today. It **will be** a fine day.

6. a) . . . won't he?
   b) . . . shall I?
   c) . . . will he?
   d) . . . won't he?
   e) . . . shan't we?
   f) . . . will she?

28 IN A DEPARTMENT STORE

1. a) They go to a department store because they want to buy some presents.
   b) Mrs Brown will buy a pair of skis.
   c) Mrs White will buy some records.
   d) She'll buy skis on the second floor.
   e) She'll buy them on the ground floor.

2. 2 skis
   1 pullover
   G soap
   B sugar
   G comb
   3 chair
   2 football
   3 table
   2 skateboard
   1 dress
   G lipstick
   B flour
   3 sideboard
   B chocolate
   1 skirt
   3 shelf
   1 coat
   2 skates
   B cocoa
   1 blouse
   G tooth-brush

3. Mrs Brown will buy soap. She'll buy it on the ground floor.
   Mrs White will buy sugar. She'll buy it at the supermarket.
   Mrs Brown will buy a comb. She'll buy it on the ground floor.
   Mrs White will buy a chair. She'll buy it on the third floor.
   Mrs Brown will buy a football. She'll buy it on the second floor.
   Mrs White will buy a table. She'll buy it on the third floor.

Mrs Brown will buy a skateboard. She'll buy it one the second floor.
Mrs White will buy a dress. She'll buy it on the first floor.
Mrs Brown will buy a lipstick. She'll buy it on the ground floor.
Mrs White will buy flour. She'll buy it at the supermarket.
Mrs Brown will buy a sideboard. She'll buy it on the third floor.
Mrs White will buy chocolate. She'll buy it at the supermarket.
Mrs Brown will buy a skirt. She'll buy it on the first floor.
Mrs White will buy a shelf. She'll buy it on the third floor.
Mrs Brown will buy a coat. She'll buy it on the first floor.
Mrs White will buy skates. She'll buy them on the second floor.
Mrs Brown will buy cocoa. She'll buy it at the supermarket.
Mrs White will buy a blouse. She'll buy it on the first floor.
Mrs Brown will buy a tooth-brush. She'll buy it on the ground floor.

4. I want a skirt for my birthday. I hope I'll get a skirt.
I want a pullover for my birthday. I hope I'll get a pullover.
I want shoes for my birthday. I hope I'll get shoes.
I want a dress for my birthday. I hope I'll get a dress.
I want boots for my birthday. I hope I'll get boots.

9 CLEARANCE SALES!
EVERYTHING'S REDUCED!

1. a) She'll go to town tomorrow.
   b) She'll buy some stools and a chair bed.
   c) Yes, there's a sale on.
   d) Yes, there is.
   e) She'll go to town tomorrow because there's a sale on.
   f) Mrs Brown will come with her.

2. Mrs White says, "Look at this bar stool!
   It's previous price was £ 14.99.
   I'll get it for £ 4.99
   £ 10 are off!"

   Mrs White says, "Look at this fold-away chair!
   It's previous price was £ 19.99
   I'll get it for £ 3.99.
   £ 16 are off!"

3. Shop-assistant: Oh, it's a prettily **patterned chair.** It's a **bed**. At this
                   price it's a giveaway!
   Mrs White: And what about your fold-away chairs?
   Shop-assistant: They're very cheap, only £ 3.99.

171

Mrs White: Are the seats made of leather?

Shop-assistant: No, it's a **red plastic seat.**

Mrs White: I'd like to have a look at the bar stools, too!

Shop-assistant: Just look at this **bar stool.** It's legs are **elegantly** carved.

Mrs White: I'll take one chair bed, four fold-away chairs and three bar stools.

Shop-assistant: That'll be **£ 50.92** altogether.

30   SHOPPING IN THE BURLINGTON ARCADES

2. a) A: Mr Miller has a new house. - And Mr Johnson?
   B: He has an old one.

   b) A: Betty likes her long coat. - And Nelly?
   B: She likes her short one.

   c) A: Mrs White bought an expensive handbag. - And Mrs Brown?
   B: She bought a cheap one.

   d) A: John got a bad mark. - And Tom?
   B: He got a good one.

   e) A: Mary wrote a long letter. - And Peter?
   B: He wrote a short one.

3. a) A: Look at these nice blouses!
   B: The green one is beautiful, but the blue ones are too expensive.

   b) A: Look at these nice cardigans!
   B: The brown one is rather cheap, but the black ones are really lovely.

   c) A: Look at these nices dresses!
   B: The white one is beautiful, but the red ones are old-fashioned.

   d) A: Look at these nice coats!
   B: The blue one is fashionable, but the red ones are too elegant.

4. Mrs Brown: Hello, Mrs White! Shopping in the Burlington Arcades?
   Mrs White: Yes, I'm after some handmade toys and a fine purse. I'm sure I'll find something beautiful in one of the 38 shops.
   Mrs Brown: Just look at this lovely doll!
   Mrs White: The big one is very nice, but the small one is too expensive for me.
   Mrs Brown: Look at these elegant purses!

Mrs White: The green ones are too small, the brown ones are lovely, indeed — but too expensive altogether!

Mrs Brown: I think we'd rather go to a department store!

1 LET'S DO THE SHOPPING!

1. At the grocer's: 2 glasses of jam, 2 jars of mustard, 2 bottles of juice, a box of sugar, 2 packets of sweets, 2 bars of chocolate
   At the greengrocer's: carrots
   At the tobacconist's: 2 packets of cigarettes
   At the butcher's: a piece of sausage, half a pound of beef

2. a) Can you tell us the way to the grocer's, please?
      We've got to buy jam.
   b) Can you tell us the way to the greengrocer's, please?
      We've got to buy carrots.
   c) Can you tell us the way to the tobacconist's, please?
      We've got to buy cigarettes.

3. A: Have you got **any** juice?
   B: Yes, we've got **some**.
   A: Then give me two bottles of juice.

   A: Have you got **any** bread?
   B: Yes, we've got **some**.
   A: Then give me two loaves of bread.

   A: Have you got **any** sweets?
   B: Yes, we've got **some**.
   A: Then give me two packets of sweets.

   A: Have you got **any** chocolate?
   B: Yes, we've got **some**.
   A: Then give me two bars of chocolate.

4. A: Have you got **any** sausage?
   B: Oh, I'm sorry, there isn't **any** sausage left.

   A: Have you got **any** beef?
   B: Oh, I'm sorry, there isn't **any** beef left.

   A: Have you got **any** sugar?
   B: Oh, I'm sorry, there isn't **any** sugar left.

   A: Have you got **any** bread?
   B: Oh, I'm sorry, there isn't **any** bread left.

A: Have you got **any** juice?

B: Oh, I'm sorry, there isn't **any** juice left.

5. a) Did you buy **any** juice? - Yes, we bought **some** juice.
Did you buy **any** bread? - Yes, we bought **some** bread.
Did you buy **any** chocolate? - Yes, we bought **some** chocolate.

b) Did you buy **any** beef? - No, we didn't buy **any** beef.
Did you buy **any** sugar? - No, we didn't buy **any** sugar.
Did you buy **any** mustard? - No, we didn't buy **any** mustard.

6. A: Two jars of mustard, please!
B: I'm sorry, there's only one jar of mustard left.

A: Two bottles of juice, please!
B: I'm sorry, there's only one bottle of juice left.

A: Two loaves of bread, please!
B: I'm sorry, there's only one loaf of bread left.

A: Two packets of sweets please!
B: I'm sorry, there's only one packet of sweets left.

A: Two bars of chocolate, please!
B: I'm sorry, there's only one bar of chocolate left.

32 WHO or WHICH?

1. a) It was Betty **who** made the beds.
b) A pen is a thing **which** we need for writing.
c) It was Jane **who** wrote the exercise.
d) It was Joe **who** broke the glasses.
e) I don't like books **which** are boring.
f) Tom saw a film **which** was interesting.
g) This is the coat **which** was very expensive.
h) It was Nelly **who** fell asleep.

2. 11 teach children
8 steer jet planes
9 type letters
10 sell fine dresses
12 serve people
7 set people's hair
6 sell sugar and flour
5 milk the cows

4 repair teeth
3 make sausages
2 drive buses
1 bake bread

3. Is a bus driver **a person who** steers jet planes?
   No, a bus driver is **a person who** drives buses.

   Is a butcher **a person who** types letters?
   No, a butcher is **a person who** makes sausages.

   Is a dentist **a person who** sells fine dresses?
   No, a dentist is **a person who** repairs teeth.

   Is a farmer **a person who** serves people?
   No, a farmer is **a person who** milks the cows.

   Is a grocer **a person who** sets people's hair?
   No, a grocer is **a person who** sells sugar and flour.

   Is a hairdresser **a person who** sells sugar and flour?
   No, a hairdresser is **a person who** sets people's hair.

   Is a pilot **a person who** milks the cows?
   No, a pilot is **a person who** steers jet planes.

   Is a secretary **a person who** repairs teeth?
   No, a secretary is **a person who** types letters.

   Is a shop-assistant **a person who** makes sausages?
   No, a shop-assistant is **a person who** sells fine dresses.

   Is a teacher **a person who** drives buses?
   No, a teacher is **a person who** teaches children.

   Is a waiter **a person who** bakes bread?
   No, a waiter is **a person who** serves people.

4. a) Peter doesn't read **books which** are boring.
   b) The cat doesn't drink **milk which** is warm.
   c) Betty can't answer **questions which** are difficult.
   d) Joe likes **tests which** are easy.
   e) Jane prefers **puzzles which** are difficult.

5. a) He took my book **which** was on the table.
   b) Here is the boy **who** wants to help you.
   c) Here is the man **who** followed me.
   d) This is Pat's brother **who** lives in New York.
   e) We'll take the train **which** arrives in Brighton at 10.30.

2. A: How do you like this black hat?
   B: Oh, I think, it doesn't suit me.

   A: How do you like this blue dress?
   B: Oh, I think, it doesn't suit me.

   A: How do you like this white skirt?
   B: Oh, I think, it doesn't suit me.

   A: How do you like this red pullover?
   B: Oh, I think, it doesn't suit me.

3. A: This green skirt doesn't fit. It's too long.
   B: That doesn't matter! We can make it shorter.

   A: This black jacket doesn't fit. It's too tight.
   B: That doesn't matter! We can make it wider.

   A: This red costume doesn't fit. It's too short.
   B: That doesn't matter! We can make it longer.

   A: This white frock doesn't fit. It's too big.
   B: That doesn't matter! We can make it smaller.

4. This black hat suits me, it fits, but it doesn't go with my pullover and my shoes.

   This red cap suits me, it fits, but it doesn't go with my pullover and my shoes.

   These green shorts suit me, they fit, but they don't go with my pullover and my shoes.

   These white socks suit me, they fit, but they don't go with my pullover and my shoes.

5. a) A: Does this skirt fit?
      B: Yes, that's the skirt which fits.

   b) A: Does this blouse fit?
      B: Yes, that's the blouse which fits.

   c) A: Does this dress fit?
      B: Yes, that's the dress which fits.

   d) A: Does this hat fit?
      B: Yes, that's the hat which fits.

e) A: Does this cap fit?
   B: Yes, that's the cap which fits.

6. Keine Angaben, individuelle Lösungsmöglichkeiten!

WHAT WAS GOING ON WHEN . . . ?

1 a) The teacher **was singing** a song when Peter **entered** the classroom.
  b) Ann **was doing** her exercises when Mum **entered** her room.
  c) Dad **was reading** the newspaper when the telephone **rang.**
  d) Sue **was playing** on the piano when Dad **opened** the door.

2. a) While Joe **was learning** English, Pat **was playing** football.
   b) While Ann **was writing** a letter, Nelly **was reading** a book.
   c) While Sue **was sleeping**, Tom **was studying** English.
   d) While Jim **was packing** his suitcase, Joe **was working** in the garden.

3. a) When the teacher came into the classroom Pat was standing on the cupboard.
   b) When the teacher came into the classroom Ann was standing on the chair.
   c) When the teacher came into the classroom Nelly was playing ball.
   d) When the teacher came into the classroom Jack and Sue were dancing.

4. a) Peter was singing a song, **wasn't he?**
   b) Joe and Jack were dancing, **weren't they?**
   c) You were playing ball, **weren't you?**
   d) Ann was writing a test, **wasn't she?**
   e) Sue and Nelly were sleeping, **weren't they?**
   f) Jane wasn't speaking English, **was she?**
   g) The children weren't learning French, **were they?**

TRY THIS TEST   UNIT 22 - 34

A. 1. d)
   2. b)
   3. a)
   4. b)
   5. b)
   6. a)
   7. b)
   8. c)

B. 1. will write
    2. shall learn
    3. will clean
    4. will bake
    5. will wash
    6. shall read
    7. will be
    8. will travel

C. 1. were playing / entered
    2. rang / was playing

D. 1. ones
    2. one
    3. ones
    4. one

E. 1. any
    2. any
    3. some
    4. some
    5. any

F. 1. who
    2. which
    3. which
    4. who
    5. which

G. 1. I'd like a skirt.
    2. What about this very nice red skirt?
    3. It's very nice but it doesn't fit.
    4. That doesn't matter, we can make it wider.

35 A MESS IN THE CLASSROOM

1. a) A: Whose pencil is this? Betty's?
      B: Yes, it's her pencil. It's hers.

   b) A: Whose pencil-case it this? Sue's?
      B: Yes, it's her pencil-case. It's hers.

   c) A: Whose copy-books are these? Ann's and John's?
      B: Yes, they're their copy-books. They're theirs.

d) A: Whose box is this? My box and Peter's?
   B: Yes, it's your box and Peter's. It's yours.

e) A: Whose book is this? John's?
   B: Yes, it's his book. It's his.

f) A: Whose ball is this? My ball and Jane's?
   B: Yes, it's your ball and Jane's. It's yours.

2. a) A: Are these pencils his or hers?
      B: I think, they're his. Hers are over there.

   b) A: Are these rubbers ours or theirs?
      B: I think, they're ours. Theirs are over there.

   c) A: Are these copy-books mine or yours?
      B: I think, they're mine. Yours are over there.

   d) A: Are these pictures yours or his?
      B: I think, they're mine. His are over there.

3. a) A: Whose pencil-sharpener is this?
      B: Which pencil-sharpener?
      A: The one in your pencil-case!
      B: It's **Peter's**. It belongs **to him**.

   b) A: Whose shoes are these?
      B: Which shoes?
      A: The ones under the table!
      B: They're **Mary's**. They belong **to her**.

   c) A: Whose box is this?
      B: Which box?
      A: The one on the table!
      B: It's **Jim's and Betty's**. It belongs **to them**.

4. A: What are you doing with those two balls?
   B: One is mine and the other is yours.
   A: Then give me mine.

   A: What are you doing with those two balls?
   B: One is mine and the other is Peter's.
   A: Then give him his.

   A: What are you doing with those two balls?
   B: One is mine and the other is Betty's.
   A: Then give her hers.

A: What are you doing with those two pullovers?
B: One is mine and the other is yours.
A: Then give me mine.

A: What are you doing with those two pullovers?
B: One is mine and the other is Peter's.
A: Then give him his.

A: What are you doing with those two pullovers?
B: One is mine and the other is Betty's.
A: Then give her hers.

A: What are you doing with those two fountain-pens?
B: One is mine and the other is yours.
A: Then give me mine.

A: What are you doing with those two fountain-pens?
B: One is mine and the other is Peter's.
A: Then give him his.

A: What are you doing with those two fountain-pens?
B: One is mine and the other is Betty's.
A: Then give her hers.

36 DIFFERENT SCHOOLS -
THE SAME LESSONS

2. A: When do you have biology?
   B: I have biology on Monday in the fifth lesson and on Saturday in the third lesson.

   A: When do you have art?
   B: I have art on Wednesday in the third and fourth lesson.

   A: When do you have geography?
   B: I have geography on Wednesday in the fifth lesson and on Friday in the fifth lesson.

   A: When do you have religious instruction?
   B: I have religious instruction on Monday in the first lesson and on Friday in the sixth lesson.

3. a) A: How often do you have orchestra a week?
      B: Once a week. We have one orchestra lesson.

   b) A: How often do you have biology a week?
      B: Twice a week. We have two biology lessons.

c) A: How often do you have history a week?
   B: Three times a week. We have three history lessons.

d) A: How often do you have maths a week?
   B: Four times a week. We have four maths lessons.

e) A: How often do you have German a week?
   B: Five times a week. We have five German lessons.

4. Keine Angaben möglich, individuelle Lösungsmöglichkeiten.

5. 1. English
    2. German
    3. History
    4. Geography
    5. Handicraft
    6. E
    7. Physics
    8. Maths
    9. Music
   10. N
   11. Biology
   School is always very **interesting**.

7 A LETTER FROM ENGLAND

1. a) No   b) No   c) Yes   d) No   e) Yes   f) No

2. a) I like history.
      I like biology **better** than history.
      I like geography **best**. It's my favorite subject.

   b) I like handicraft.
      I like physical education **better** than handicraft.
      I like physics **best**. It's my favourite subject.

   c) I like religious instruction.
      I like English **better** than religious instruction.
      I like maths **best**. It's my favourite subject.

   d) I like art.
      I like music **better** than art.
      I like history **best**. It's my favourite subject.

3. a) Ann likes English because it is useful.
      She hates physics because it is difficult.

   b) Sue and Ellen like art because it is great fun.
      They hate maths because it is useless.

   c) Pat likes geography because it is interesting.
      He hates history because it is not important.

   d) I like . . .
      I hate . . .

4. Keine Angaben, individuelle Lösungsmöglichkeiten

5. Tom: What's your favourite subject?
   Sue: I like English best.
   Tom: Why do you like English best?
   Sue: English is interesting, useful and not difficult.

38 HAVE YOU DONE YOUR EXERCISES YET?

2. | you bring | you brought | you have brought |
   |-----------|-------------|------------------|
   | he comes | he came | he has come |
   | she does | she did | she has done |
   | we drink | we drank | we have drunk |
   | you eat | you ate | you have eaten |
   | they find | they found | they have found |
   | I get | I got | I have got |
   | you give | you gave | you have given |
   | he makes | he made | he has made |
   | she reads | she read | she has read |

3. a) A: **Have** you **eaten** your bread yet?
      B: Yes, of course! **I've** already **eaten** it.

   b) A: Have you **drunk** your tea yet?
      B: Yes, of course! **I've** already **drunk** it.

   c) A: Have you **cleaned** your room yet?
      B: Yes, of course! **I've** already **cleaned** it.

4. a) A: Are you doing your homework?
      B: **I've** already **done** my homework.

   b) A: Are you writing a letter to Granny?
      B: **I've** already **written** a letter to Granny.

   c) A: Are you learning your new words?
      B: **I've** already **learned** my new words.

5. a) A: When will Peter do his homework?
      B: He **has** just **done** his homework.

   b) A: When will Peter write a letter to Granny?
      B: He **has** just **written** a letter to Granny.

   c) A: When will Peter learn his new words?
      B: He **has** just **learned** his new words.

SIGHTSEEING IN LONDON

1. a) Jim is speaking English.
      Have you ever spoken English?

   b) Pat is asking a policeman.
      Have you ever asked a policeman?

   c) Joe is driving a car.
      Have you ever driven a car?

   d) Sue is running to the station.
      Have you ever run to the station?

   e) Sandy is drinking whisky.
      Have you ever drunk whisky?

2. a) A: Look at the National Gallery!
         Have you ever seen such an interesting museum?
      B: No, I've never seen such an interesting museum!

   b) A: Look at the Tower!
         Have you ever seen such an old castle?
      B: No, I've never seen such an old castle!

   c) A: Look at St. Martin's-in-the Fields!
         Have you ever seen such an interesting church?
      B: No, I've never seen such an interesting church.

3. a) A: We've just seen a film. I's very exciting.
   B· I've never seen such an exciting film. It's the most exciting film
      I've ever seen.

   b) A: We've just eaten an ice-cream. It's very fine.
      B: I've never eaten such a fine ice-cream. It's the finest ice-cream
         I've ever eaten.

   c) A: We've just crossed Oxford Street. It's very busy.
      B: I've never seen such a busy street. It's the busiest street I've ever
         seen.

   d) A: We've just watched "Changing the Guard". It's very funny.
      B: I've never watched such a funny spectacle. It's the funniest
         spectacle I've ever watched.

4. A: Joe, have you ever seen such an interesting bridge?
   B: No, I haven't. I've never seen such an interesting bridge.
      It's really the most interesting bridge I've ever seen.

40 EVERYTHING HERE'S SECOND-HAND!

1. a) No   b) No   c) No   d) Yes   e) No   f) Yes   g) Yes

2. a) Nelly didn't want her ball, so she brought her ball.
   b) Joe didn't want his toy train, so he brought his toy train.
   c) Frank didn't want his toy car, so he brought his toy car.
   d) Sue and Ann didn't want their camera, so they brought their
      camera.

3. a) A: Just have a look at this funny kite!
      B: I've never seen a funnier one.
      A: Yes, it's really the funniest kite I've ever seen.

   b) A: Just have a look at this nice lamp!
      B: I've never seen a nicer one.
      A: Yes, it's really the nicest lamp I've ever seen.

   c) A: Just have a look at this nice toy car!
      B: I've never seen a nicer one.
      A: Yes, it's really the nicest toy car I've ever seen.

   d) A: Just have a look at this beautiful chess set!
      B: I've never seen a more beautiful one.
      A: Yes, it's really the most beautiful chess set I've ever seen.

4. a) No, he hasn't.
   b) Yes, I have.
   c) Yes, she has.
   d) No, he hasn't.
   e) No, she hasn't.

5. a) Peter hasn't bought anything, **has he**?
   b) You have brought the toy train, **haven't you?**
   c) Mary has brought the doll, **hasn't she?**
   d) Tom and Joe haven't bought anything, **have they**?
   e) Jim has bought a ball, **hasn't he?**

1 SKIING IN SPRING

1. I'll <u>do</u> it slowly . . .
   I can <u>ski</u> well.
   I can <u>stop</u> quickly.

2. a) Tom runs **quickly**. He is a **quick** runner.
   b) Peter is a **polite** boy. He greets **politely**.
   c) Ann skis **badly**. She is a **bad** skier.
   d) Jane is a **beautiful** girl. But she doesn't sing **beautifully.**
   e) Skiing is **easy**. Tom learned it **easily**.
   f) Fred is a **fast** skier. Yes, he skis **fast**.
   g) Sue is a **good** girl. She can't ski **well.**

3. a) Joe **hardly** goes to football matches.
   b) Dad works **hard**.
   c) His friend **hardly** works.
   d) Are the children working **hard**?

4. a) Pat **nearly** missed the bus.
   b) Ann lives **near** the theatre.
   c) Uncle Fred **nearly** visited us.
   d) Dad **nearly** bought that expensive car.

5. a) Are you **late** for school?
   b) I haven't been to the theatre **lately**.
   c) Joe arrived **late** last Sunday.
   d) We haven't talked to him **lately**.

42 A COMPETITION

1. beautifully - more beautifully - most beautifully
   fast - faster - fastest
   well - better - best
   quickly - more quickly - most quickly
   badly - more badly - most badly
   slowly - more slowly - most slowly

2. Reporter:
   Let's have a look at the girls!
   Ann is skiing **slowly**, not quickly.
   Alice is skiing **more slowly**.
   And what about Ellen? — Where is she?
   Oh, she's skiing **most slowly** of all!
   What a pity! All the girls are skiing too slowly to win a prize.

   And what about the boys?
   Jim is skiing **quickly**.
   Joe is skiing **more quickly**.
   John is skiing **most quickly** of all!
   He is the winner.

3. a) Who ran most slowly?
      Sue ran slowly.
      Betty ran more slowly.
      Sandy ran most slowly.

   b) Who skated best?
      Jim skated well.
      Joe skated better.
      Ann skated best.

   c) Who played worst?
      Jim played badly.
      Joe played worse.
      John played worst.

4. a) Who ran most slowly? It was Sandy who ran most slowly.
   b) Who skated best? It was Ann who skated best.
   c) Who played worst? It was John who played worst.

5. a) Why did Pat win the competition?
      Because he ran most quickly.

b) Why did Ann get a good mark?
   Because she wrote the exercise most carefully.

c) Why did Sue get a bad mark?
   Because she painted the picture worst.

d) Why did Joe arrive in time?
   Because he got up earliest.

e) Why did Jim kiss the snow?
   Because he skied most carelessly.

3 A NEW PUPIL

1. She is from **Yugoslavia**.
   Anica lived in **Belgrade**.
   She has got two **brothers**.
   She stayed in Graz three **years** ago.
   She speaks **English** quite well.

2. a) A: Have you ever been to Reading before?
      B: No, never. But four months ago I stayed in Oxford.

   b) A: Have you ever been to Innsbruck before?
      B: No, never. But two years ago I stayed in Schwaz.

   c) A: Have you ever been to Paris before?
      B: No, never. But five years ago I stayed in Nice.

   d) A: Have you ever been to Munich before?
      B: No, never. But six weeks ago I stayed in Rosenheim.

3. a) A: You speak English quite well!
      B: But I'm afraid my English won't be good enough to understand
         the people in London.
   b) A: You speak Italian quite well!
      B: But I'm afraid my Italian won't be good enough to understand
         the people in Rome.
   c) A: You speak Greek quite well!
      B: But I'm afraid my Greek won't be good enough to understand
         the people in Athens.
   d) A: You speak Spanish quite well!
      B: But I'm afraid my Spanish won't be good enough to
         understand the people in Madrid.

187

4. There's a new pupil in our class.
   She came from Yugoslavia.
   Her name is Anica Kostič.
   She has got two brothers but no sister.
   She speaks English quite well.

44 HOW TO MAKE A CAKE

1. Unterstreiche: put, beat, put, beat, pour, beat, fill, put, take

2. to put - put - put
   to beat - beat - beaten
   to pour - poured - poured
   to fill - filled - filled
   to take - took - taken

3. When you have beaten them with your electric beater, you put the eggs into the basin.
   When you have put the eggs into the basin, you beat them.
   When you have beaten them, you pour the flour and the baking-powder into the basin.
   When you have poured the flour and the baking-powder into the basin, you beat them.
   When you have beaten them, you fill the tin from the basin.
   When you have filled the tin from the basin, you put it into the oven.
   When you have put it into the oven you take the cake out after 35 minutes.

4. Tom: Have you already beaten them with your electric beater?
   Joe: I've just beaten them with my electric beater.

   Tom: Have you already put the eggs into the basin?
   Joe: I've just put the eggs into the basin.

   Tom: Have you already beaten them?
   Joe: I've just beaten them.

   Tom: Have you already poured the flour and the baking-powder into the basin?
   Joe: I've just poured the flour and the baking-powder into the basin.

   Tom: Have you already filled the tin from the basin?
   Joe: I've just filled the tin from the basin.

Tom: Have you already put it into the oven?
Joe: I've just put it into the oven.

Tom: Have you already taken the cake out?
Joe: I've just taken the cake out.

5. Tom: Have you beaten them with your electric beater?
Joe: No, I have forgotten to beat them with my electric beater.

Tom: Have you put the eggs into the basin?
Joe: No, I have forgotten to put them into the basin.

Tom: Have you beaten them?
Joe: No, I have forgotten to beat them.

Tom: Have you poured the flour and the baking-powder into the basin?
Joe: No, I have forgotten to pour the flour and the baking-powder into the basin.

Tom: Have you filled the tin from the basin?
Joe: No, I have forgotten to fill the tin from the basin.

Tom: Have you put it into the oven?
Joe: No, I have forgotten to put it into the oven.

Tom: Have you taken the cake out?
Joe: No, I have forgotten to take the cake out.

6. A: Have you ever eaten such a fine cake?
B: No, I've never eaten such a fine cake.

A: Have you ever prepared such a fine cake?
B: No, I've never prepared such a fine cake.

A: Have you ever tried such a fine cake?
B: No, I've never tried such a fine cake.

A: Have you ever smelled such a fine cake?
B: No, I've never smelled such a fine cake.

A: Have you ever tasted such a fine cake?
B: No, I've never tasted such a fine cake.

A: Have you ever got such a fine cake?
B: No, I've never got such a fine cake.

7. a) No   b) No   c) Yes   d) No   e) No

45 IT'S THE BEST FILM THAT I'VE EVER SEEN

1. a) A: Can you come to the "Coliseum" with me tonight?
      "La Traviata" is the best opera that I've ever seen!
   B: That's really a good idea! But I wanted to watch "The Secret
      Servant". It's the best film that I've ever seen. Everything that is
      on TV 1 is interesting.

   b) A: Can you come to "Convent Garden" with me tonight?
      "Swan Lake" is the best ballet that I've ever seen!
   B: That's really a good idea! But I wanted to watch "Paul
      McCartney". It's the best documentary that I've ever seen.
      Everything that is on TV 1 is interesting.

2. a) A: Is this play amusing? Have you seen it?
   B: Yes, it's the **most amusing** play **that** I've ever seen.

   b) A: Is this book boring? Have you read it?
   B: Yes, it's the **most boring** book **that** I've ever read.

   c) A: Is this story funny? Have you heard it?
   B: Yes, it's the **funniest** story **that** I've ever heard.

   d) A: Is this puzzle difficult? Have you tried it?
   B: Yes, it's the **most difficult** puzzle **that** I've ever tried.

3. a) Mr Miller bought everything **that** was on sale.
   b) Here is the boy **who** won the first prize.
   c) They were looking for the book **which** was on the shelf.
   d) This is the most interesting story **that** I have ever read.
   e) This is the present **which** I bought for Nelly.
   f) Yes, it's the most expensive present **that** I've ever bought.
   g) Is there anything **that** we can do for you?
   h) This is the girl **who** sang the beautiful songs.
   i) This is the most beautiful girl **that** I have ever seen.
   j) All **that** he said was true.

4. Individuelle Lösungsmöglichkeiten.

A. 1. has written
   2. have baked
   3. have learned
   4. have drunk
   5. have read
   6. has watched
   7. has eaten
   8. have washed

B. 1. hers
   2. theirs
   3. mine
   4. ours
   5. mine
   6. his

C. 1. easy / easily
   2. fast / fast
   3. well / good
   4. bad / badly
   5. slowly / slow
   6. in a friendly way / friendly

D. 1. late
   2. lately
   3. hardly
   4. hard
   5. nearly
   6. near

E. 1. who
   2. that
   3. that
   4. that
   5. which
   6. that
   7. who
   8. that

F. 1. How often do you have geography a week?
   2. Twice a week.
   3. Franz, I'd like to have a look at your time-table.
   4. Oh, look! We've just the same lessons!

1. If I had a lot of money, I'd buy a house.
   If I had a lot of money, I'd travel round the world.
   If I had a lot of money, I'd buy a horse.
   If I had a lot of money, I'd help the poor.

   If I were rich, I'd buy a house.
   If I were rich, I'd travel round the world.
   If I were rich, I'd buy a horse.
   If I were rich, I'd help the poor.

2. If Tom were rich, he'd buy a house.
   If Tom had time, he'd go to the cinema.
   If Tom had time, he'd play tennis.
   If Tom had time, he'd go to the theatre.

   If Ann were rich, she'd buy a house.
   If Ann had time, she'd play tennis.
   If Ann had time, she'd go to the cinema.
   If Ann had time, she'd go to the theatre.

   If we were rich, we'd buy a house.
   If we had time, we'd play tennis.
   If we had time, we'd go to the theatre.
   If we had time, we'd go to the cinema.

3. a) If we had time, we could go to the cinema.
   b) If Tom were at school, he could meet his friends.
   c) If I were rich, I could buy a car.
   d) If Betty were in the garden, she could play ball.

4. a) A: Can he win the prize? Is he really so fast?
      B: If he were fast, he'd win the prize.

   b) A: Can she ski down the slope? Is she really so courageous?
      B: If she were courageous, she'd ski down the slope.

   c) A: Can he play the piano? Is he really so musical?
      B: If he were musical, he'd play the piano.

   d) A: Can she carry that sack? Is she really so strong?
      B: If she were strong, she'd carry that sack.

1.

P	D	
X		You must not play ...
X		Don't use ...
		Don't cycle ...
X	X	You must not ...
X	X	Don't go ...
X	X	Don't forget ...
X		Don't read ...
	X	You must not overtake ...
X	X	Don't cross ...

2. A: Mum, I want to go out!
   B: All right! But don't play in the street!
      You must not play in the street!

   A: Mum, I want to go out!
   B: All right! But don't use your skateboard on the road!
      You must not use your skateboard on the road!

   A: Mum, I want to go out!
   B: All right! But don't cycle on the wrong side of the road!
      You must not cycle on the wrong side of the road!

   A: Mum, I want to go out!
   B: All right! But don't go when the sign says "STOP"!
      You must not go when the sign says "STOP"!

3. What does this traffic sign tell us?
   a) It says, "You must not turn right!"
   b) It says, "You must not overtake other cars!"
   c) It says, "You must not stop here!"
   d) It says, "You must not drive fast!"

4. a) You may use your skateboard in the park, but you must not use it on the road.
   b) You may cross the road when the traffic light is green, but you must not cross the road when the traffic light is red or amber.
   c) You may cycle on the left side of the road, but you must not cycle on the right side of the road.
   d) You may go when the traffic light says "GO", but you must not go when the traffic light says "STOP".
   e) You may walk on the pavement, but you must not walk on the road.

5. a) You are a **quick** boy. Cross the road **quickly**.
   b) You must drive **carefully** here! Don't forget to be **careful**!
   c) Look **carefully!** You must be **careful** when you cross the road.
   d) Look right and left, then run **quickly**! Be **quick**.
   e) Drive **slowly** at the beginning! You must be **slow** here!

48 OUR NEW HOUSE

1. A: Must we vacuum the floor now?
   B: Yes, you have to vacuum it now.

   A: Must we wash the glasses now?
   B: Yes, you have to wash them now.

   A: Must we paint the windows now?
   B: Yes, you have to paint them now.

   A: Must we dust the chairs now?
   B: Yes, you have to dust the chairs now.

   A: Must we polish the floor now?
   B: Yes, you have to polish the floor now.

2. A: Must we vacuum the floor now?
   B: Oh no, you don't have to vacuum the floor now.

   A: Must we wash the glasses now?
   B: Oh no, you don't have to wash the glasses now.

   A: Must we paint the windows now?
   B: Oh no, you don't have to paint the windows now.

   A: Must we dust the chairs now?
   B: Oh no, you don't have to dust the chairs now.

   A: Must we polish the floor now?
   B: On no, you don't have to polish the floor now.

3. a) Yesterday I had to paper the living room.
      Today I have to paper the bed room.

   b) Yesterday I had to clean the windows.
      Today I have to clean the doors.

   c) Yesterday I had to vacuum the floor.
      Today I have to vacuum the armchairs.

   d) Yesterday I had to wash the glasses.
      Today I have to wash the pots and pans.

e) Yesterday I had to install the fuse boxes.
Today I have to install the water-taps.

4. a) Today Joe has to paper the living room.
Yesterday he had to paper the bed room.

b) Today Joe has to clean the windows.
Yesterday he had to clean the doors.

c) Today Joe has to vacuum the floor.
Yesterday he had to vacuum the armchairs.

d) Today Joe has to wash the glasses.
Yesterday he had to wash the pots and pans.

e) Today Joe has to install the fuse boxes.
Yesterday he had to install the water-taps.

5. a) You must wash the cups, but you need not wash the glasses.
b) You must polish the floor, but you need not polish the furniture.
c) You must vacuum the staircase, but you need not vacuum the armchairs.
d) You must dust the furniture, but you need not dust the windows.

9 LET'S HELP THE FARMER!

2. A: Jim, you can feed the hens!
B: I'm sorry, I can't feed the hens, I'm really not able to feed the hens!

A: Jim, you can bring in the hay!
B: I'm sorry, I can't bring in the hay, I'm really not able to bring in the hay!

A: Jim, you can repair the tractor!
B: I'm sorry, I can't repair the tractor, I'm really not able to repair the tractor!

A: Jim, you can clean the harvester!
B: I'm sorry, I can't clean the harvester, I'm really not able to clean the harvester!

A: Jim, you can clean the cowshed!
B: I'm sorry, I can't clean the cowshed, I'm really not able to clean the cowshed!

3. Last summer little Tom couldn't feed the hens.
   This summer he can feed them.

   Last summer little Tom couldn't bring in the hay.
   This summer he can bring in the hay.

   Last summer little Tom couldn't repair the tractor.
   This summer he can repair the tractor.

   Last summer little Tom couldn't clean the harvester.
   This summer he can clean the harvester.

   Last summer little Tom couldn't clean the cowshed.
   This summer he can clean the cowshed.

4. Nelly was able to feed the hens.
   Can you feed the hens?

   Nelly was able to bring in the hay.
   Can you bring in the hay?

   Nelly was able to repair the tractor.
   Can you repair the tractor?

   Nelly was able to clean the harvester.
   Can you clean the harvester?

   Nelly was able to clean the cowshed.
   Can you clean the cowshed?

5. a) Last summer Uncle Fred **could not** bring in the hay.
   b) Little Tom **isn't able to** reach the apples, he isn't tall enough.
   c) Aunt Betty **can't** clean the sty today.
   d) Yesterday she **wasn't able to** clean the sty.
   e) All the children **can** help the farmer.
   f) Uncle Fred **wasn't able to** repair the tractor.

50 JOE'S BIRTHDAY - A DAY OF BAD LUCK!

1. a) No   b) Yes   c) No   d) No   e) No   f) Yes

2. a) A: Joe can get up.
      B: I bet Joe isn't able to get up.

   b) A: Joe can play tennis.
      B: I bet Joe isn't able to play tennis.

   c) A: Joe can go boating.
      B: I bet Joe isn't able to go boating.

d) A: Joe can come with us.
   B: I bet Joe isn't able to come with us.

e) A: Joe can help us.
   B: I bet Joe isn't able to help us.

3. a) A: He could not get up.
      B: Why was he not able to get up?

   b) A: He could not play football.
      B: Why was he not able to play football?

   c) A: He could not go to school.
      B: Why was he not able to go to school?

   d) A: He could not practise roller-skating.
      B: Why was he not able to practise roller-skating.

   e) A: He could not come with us.
      B: Why was he not able to come with us?

4. a) . . . must not . . .
   b) . . . must . . .
   c) . . . must . . .
   d) . . . must not . . .
   e) . . . must not . . .

5. Dear Jack,
   My greatest wish was to get roller-skates for my 12th birthday. So Dad
   bought roller-skates and a safety equipment: a helmet and knee pads
   for me.
   When I got my birthday presents I was so happy that I tried the roller-
   skates out at once.
   But I forgot something very important: I didn't put on my helmet and
   I didn't take my knee pads.
   I went to the park - the new roller-skates were fantastic! Suddenly
   two big dogs came out from behind the trees. I couldn't stop - I fell!
   I hurt my knees and elbows so that I wasn't able to get up. An
   ambulance took me to hospital.
   My 12th birthday - a day of bad luck!

2. a) No   b) Yes   c) No   d) No   e) No   f) No   g) No

3. He didn't pick some flowers.
   There were plastic bags.
   There was no refuse bin.
   They didn't arrive at a river. They arrived at a lake.
   The water was not very fine.
   They came home earlier than usual.

4. A: Let's throw away the plastic bags!
   B: No, you must not throw away the plastic bags.

   A: Let's throw away the empty tins!
   B: No, you must not throw away the empty tins.

   A: Let's throw away the paper bags!
   B: No, you must not throw away the paper bags.

5. A: Did you throw away the plastic bags?
   B: No, I didn't.

   A: Did you throw away the empty tins?
   B: No, I didn't.

   A: Did you throw away the paper bags?
   B: No, I didn't.

6. A: Why did you throw away the plastic bags?
   B: Sorry, I'll collect them and put them into the refuse bin.

   A: Why did you throw away the empty tins?
   B: Sorry, I'll collect them and put them into the refuse bin.

   A: Why did you throw away the paper bags?
   B: Sorry, I'll collect them and put them into the refuse bin.

52 LET'S HAVE A PARTY!

1. Beispiele:

   Let's invite all our friends!
   Yes, that's a good idea!
   It would be fine to have some orange juice.
   I don't like that!

Perhaps we could invite all our teachers!
No, that's nonsense!
We should prepare sandwiches!
That's stupid!

I think we could organize a match!
Oh, yes, let's do that!
We could make a cake
Oh, fantastic!

2. Last summer the children **invited** all their friends.
   Next summer the children **will invite** all their friends, too.

   Last summer the children **organized** a match.
   Next summer the children **will organize** a match, too.

   Last summer the children **prepared** sandwiches.
   Next summer the children **will prepare** sandwiches, too.

   Last summer the children **made** a cake.
   Next summer the children **will make** a cake, too.

   Last summer the children **had** orange juice.
   Next summer the children **will have** orange juice, too.

3. We could prepare some coffee.
   We could prepare some sandwiches.
   We could prepare some juice.
   We could prepare some cake.

   Let's have some coffee.
   Let's have some sandwiches.
   Let's have some juice.
   Let's have some cake.

4. Hello, (fill in your friend's name) this is Tom speaking.
   Can you come to our party?
   Oh, yes, **that's a good idea.** When **can I come?**
   Next Monday, 6 o'clock.
   Where **will you have your party?**
   At school, in our classroom.
   That's really **a good idea.** I'd like **to come.**
   Thank you! **Bye, bye!**
   So long!

5. a) Perhaps we could prepare some sandwiches.
   b) Let's invite the Millers!
   c) We should prepare some juice!

53 TIME FOR PACKING

1. a) Nelly is sitting **between** Tom and Peter.
   b) Where are my pencils? They are **in** your pencil-case.
   c) I haven't spoken English **since** Monday.
   d) We go **to** school **by** bus.
   e) This book is very interesting. Yes, it's a book **about** London.
   f) Jim is sitting in front of Joe. Joe is **behind** Jim.
   g) Can you come **on** Sunday?
   h) We haven't spoken English **for** three days.

2. a) Who is that man **beside** you?
      That's Mr White. His wife is **behind** me.
   b) The children aren't **at** school.
      They are **at** home.
   c) I haven't watched TV **for** days.
      The programme **on** Sunday was not so bad.
   d) I've bought a book **about** Austria.
      But I can't find it. I must look **for** it.
   e) I'm looking forward **to** my holidays.
      We'll travel **to** England.

3. a) I haven't seen him **for** five days.
   b) I haven't met the Millers **since** June 3rd.
   c) We haven't been in London **for** 3 years.
   d) The Coopers haven't been in London **since** 1980.
   e) Jim has been in Italy **since** 1968.
   f) Mary has been in Greece **for** two weeks.

54 OUR FIRST BREAKFAST IN ENGLAND

2. Oh, I'm sorry, there are only a few apples left.
   I didn't buy many apples yesterday.

   Oh, I'm sorry, there are only a few oranges left.
   I didn't buy many oranges yesterday.

   Oh, I'm sorry, there are only a few peaches left.
   I didn't buy many peaches yesterday.

Oh, I'm sorry, there are only a few apricots left.
I didn't buy many apricots yesterday.

3. There is not much bacon left.
Just a little bacon is in the kitchen.

There is not much jam left.
Just a little jam is in the kitchen.

There is not much juice left.
Just a little juice is in the kitchen.

There is not much milk left.
Just a little milk is in the kitchen.

4. a) **many** eggs, **much / a lot of** water, **much / a lot of** wine, **many** bottles of wine, **many** cups of tea, **much / a lot of** bread, **many** loaves of bread, **much / a lot of** juice, **many** bottles of juice, **many** glasses of water, **much / a lot of** coffee, **many** cups of coffee, **much / a lot of** ham, **many** slices of ham, ...

   b) **a few** eggs, **little** water, **little** wine, **a few** bottles of wine, **a few** cups of tea, **little** bread, **a few** loaves of bread, **little** juice, **a few** bottles of juice, **a few** glasses of water, **little** coffee, **a few** cups of coffee, **little** ham, **a few** slices of ham, ...

5. Aunt Mary: Would you like coffee?
   Betty: I'd like some coffee — just a little.
   Aunt Mary: Would you like a piece of cake?
   Tom: No, thank you!
   Aunt Mary: Would you like some bread and rolls?
   Tom: I'd like a roll.

5 IN AN ENGLISH RESTAURANT

1. a) A: Are all these main courses here marvellous?
      B: Yes, each of these main courses here is marvellous.

   b) A: Are all these cakes here excellent?
      B: Yes, each of these cakes here is excellent.

   c) A: Are all these vegetables here fine?
      B: Yes, each of these vegetables here is fine.

   d) A: Are all these fruit tarts here sweet?
      B: Yes, each of these fruit tarts here is sweet.

2. a) Every cat has a tail.
   Each of these cats has long ears.

   b) Every house has a door.
   Each of these houses has 20 windows.

   c) Every elephant has big ears.
   Each of these elephants has a long tail.

   d) Every Englishman has an umbrella.
   Each of these Englishmen has a black umbrella.

3. a) **Every** monkey has a long tail.
   b) **Each** monkey here has a very long tail.
   c) **Every** house has a chimney.
   d) **Each of** these houses has two chimneys.
   e) **Each of** these men is a teacher.
   f) **Each of** these women here is a shop-assistant.
   g) **Every** Englishman is polite.
   h) **Each of** these men here is impolite.

4. Uncle Fred: Waiter, the menu, please!
   Betty: Oh, each of these soups is 95p.
   Uncle Fred: That's funny! Look, Betty! Each of these main
                courses is £ 3.95.

TRY THIS TEST   UNIT 46 - 55

A. 1. c)
   2. b)
   3. a)
   4. b)
   5. a)
   6. b)
   7. a)
   8. c)

B. 1. had
   2. would go
   3. were
   4. would go

C. 1. behind
   2. beside
   3. since
   4. at

5. for
6. at
7. about
8. for
9. since
10. for

D. 1. much
2. many
3. a lot of
4. little
5. few
6. few

E. 1. Every
2. Each of
3. Each of
4. Every
5. Every
6. Each of

F. 1. That's a good idea.
2. We could invite all our friends.
3. We could prepare a cake.
4. Yes, let's do that!

Renate Seebauer
Nachhilfe Englisch 1

218 Seiten, brosch., ISBN 3-85157-046-4

Unter Berücksichtigung der neuen Lehrpläne für die Hauptschulen und allgemeinbildenden höheren Schulen in Österreich trägt dieses Übungsbuch den internationalen Tendenzen im Fremdsprachenunterricht voll Rechnung.

Ausgang jeder der 60 Übungseinheiten ist der aktive Sprachgebrauch: Beschreiben, erzählen, vergleichen, Zustimmung oder Ablehnung ausdrücken, Wünsche, Absichten, Gefühle kundtun ...

Für den aktiven Gebrauch einer Fremdsprache ist die Beherrschung grundlegender grammatikalischer Strukturen Voraussetzung: don't..., doesn't..., do you...?, when does he...? Diese Verquickung „aktiver Sprachgebrauch" — „grundlegende grammatikalische Strukturen" ist das Grundkonzept von NACHHILFE ENGLISCH 1.

Der Einstieg in die Übungseinheit erfolgt in den meisten Fällen über einen Dialog der kommunikativ relevant ist und vom Schüler sofort in seinen aktiven Sprachgebrauch integriert werden kann.

Im Anschluß daran findet sich eine Vielzahl von Übungen, in welchen die im Dialog vorhandenen grammatikalischen Strukturen schrittweise aufgearbeitet werden. Alle Übungen sind so angelegt, daß sie sowohl mündlich als auch schriftlich in Einzel-, Partner- oder Gruppenarbeit durchgeführt werden können.

NACHHILFE ENGLISCH 1 gestattet vielfältige Einsatzmöglichkeiten:

— Das häusliche Üben und Wiederholen wird sinnvoll unterstützt.
— Der schulische Förderunterricht wird um eine Vielzahl von Übungsmöglichkeiten bereichert.
— Durch die ausgeführten Lösungen erhält der Schüler eine Rückmeldung über seinen Leistungsstand.

In NACHHILFE ENGLISCH 1 wird der Lehrstoff der 5. Schulstufe erarbeitet. Zum Wiederholen und Festigen des bereits Erlernten wird das Buch jedoch auch bei Schülern und Lehrern höherer Schulstufen Verwendung finden.

Verlag Leitner Wien

Renate Seebauer / Kurt Rovina
Grammatiktraining Englisch

220 Seiten, brosch., ISBN 3-85157-041-3

Im Zuge eines kontinuierlichen Lernprozesses ergibt sich immer wieder die Forderung nach einem einfach, verständlich und übersichtlich gestalteten Lernbehelf, aus dem in leicht faßbarer Form die wichtigsten Grundregeln der englischen Grammatik ersichtlich und anwendbar sind.

Bei Erstellung des vorliegenden „Trainings" stand nicht deren Vollständigkeit im Vordergrund, sondern Praxisnähe und leichte Anwendbarkeit. Kapitel aus der englischen Grammatik, die immer wieder Schwierigkeiten bereiten, werden behandelt.

Durch die textliche Gegenüberstellung deutsch-englisch sind auch wenig Geübte in der Lage, dieses „Training" durchzuführen.

Bei der Erstellung der im Anhang befindlichen Übungsaufgaben wurde besonders darauf geachtet, daß jedes Beispiel auch im direkten Sprachgebrauch verwendbar ist. Durch die angeschlossenen Lösungen ist jederzeit eine Selbstkontrolle möglich.

Die Einsatzmöglichkeiten dieses „Trainings" erstrecken sich von einer Unterstützung beim Selbststudium über Schularbeitsvorbereitung und Aufgabenhilfe bis hin zur Erleichterung des Übertrittes in eine weiterführende Schule.

Verlag Leitner Wien

Renate Seebauer / Kurt Rovina
Gesprächstraining Englisch

192 Seiten, brosch., ISBN 3-85157-045-6

Berufswelt, Alltag und Schule erfordern in erhöhtem Ausmaß von jedem einzelnen vermehrte Kommunikationsbereitschaft. Dies wiederum verlangt die Beherrschung elementarer Sprechsituationen.

Das vorliegende „Gesprächstraining" führt in übersichtlicher und allgemein verständlicher Form zu sprachrichtigem Verhalten und somit zu mehr Mobilität und Erfolg. Auf Grund der vielen Variationsmöglichkeiten wird in frei wählbarer, differenzierter Form der Aufbau kommunikativer Fähigkeiten erreicht.

Das gesamte „Trainingsprogramm" umfaßt 36 Standardsituationen, wie z.B.: Asking the way, booking a room at a hotel, travelling by car, at a restaurant.

Die Vielfalt der trainierten Sprechsituationen gewährleistet deren unmittelbare Anwendbarkeit in Schule, Freizeit und Beruf.

Der Aufbau des Werkes ist so gestaltet, daß sowohl Schüler aller Schultypen als auch Erwachsene im Selbststudium damit problemlos und erfolgreich arbeiten können.

Verlag Leitner Wien